Author and Creative Director: Andrea Hungerford
Photographer and Editor: Karen DeWitz
Pattern Designers: Thea Colman, Andrea Hungerford, Michele Lee Bernstein,
Nele Redweik, Jenn Steingass
Models: Bentlee Ewers, Lisa Ewers, Quinn Ewers, Ellery Pearson, Nele Redweik,
Charlotte Roehm
Patterns Technical Editor: Alexandra Viegel
Marketing and Social Media: Hannah Thiessen
Map Artist: Peggy Dean
Printer: B&B Print Source

ORDERING INFORMATION
By Hand is published three times annually. Subscriptions or single-issue
purchases can be ordered online at: www.byhandserial.com.

Wholesale inquiries may be submitted via e-mail to www.nnkpress.com.

Published by Blueberry Hill
www.byhandserial.com
info@byhandserial.com

PRINTED IN THE USA
This book is printed on Forest Stewardship Council® certified paper.
FSC® certification ensures that the paper in this publication contains
fibers from well managed and responsibly harvested forests that meet
strict environmental and socioeconomic standards.

FIRST EDITION
Fall 2017

making communities

Lookbook No. 4: Puget Sound

Table Of Contents

Puget Sound

Water, water everywhere! As we made our way through Puget Sound, water was a dominating force in every town or countryside. It's truly an aquaphile's dream destination. In Snoqualmie, we found waterfalls—Snoqualmie Falls, Twin Falls, and many other little waterfalls accessible by wooded hiking trails. As we drove up through the Skagit Valley, we followed a series of rivers north—the Snoqualmie, the Tolt, and the Skagit River—all the way to Bellingham. The town of Bellingham itself is all about water; it sits on the shores of Bellingham Bay overlooking the San Juan Islands. Our next few days were spent on islands, surrounded by water. On Whidbey Island, we looked out over Saratoga Passage and Penn Cove. On Bainbridge Island, we watched bald eagles hunt for their evening meal over Eagle Harbor. We traveled across the water by ferry to get to Seattle, where the city's waterfront looks out over Elliott Bay to the Olympic Mountains in one direction, and Mt. Rainer in the other.

All of our watery vistas brought with them a kaleidoscope of colors—soft pastel sunrises, bright Kodachrome sunsets, softly muted fogs, silvery gray low-hanging clouds, and purple black rain bursts. The waterfalls, the rivers, the bays and passages, the rainfall and fog—so many kinds of water in so many different permutations! Just like the Eskimos have 100 words to describe snow, I feel like Puget Sound needs at least 100 ways to describe water in all of its many forms and colors.

This presence of water, blended with the natural beauty of the fields and conifer forests, inform many of the designs and color palettes of the makers we met. Seattle, the Snoqualmie area, Mount Vernon and the Skagit valley, Bellingham, Whidbey and Bainbridge and many of the other islands in the Puget Sound region, are unquestionably home to a cluster of creatives, and the nature of what they create feels very entwined with the natural environment that surrounds and inspires them.

I have to admit my bias here: of all of the places I have lived and traveled, Puget Sound is one of those I love most. I find it so naturally beautiful. It stirs my soul, inspires me, and brings peace to my heart. If you have not yet had a chance to visit this part of the country, I encourage you to put it on your bucket list of makers' travel tours!

Making Communities

Like many knitters, I have my favorites. Favorite designers, whose sweater designs fit me well, whose sweater styles and shapes work for my body type, and whose patterns I enjoy knitting. Favorite yarns, that feel like visiting with old friends every time I knit with them. And I think we all have favorite colors. Who among us hasn't looked in their closet and said, *why does it seem like all of my handknits are in shades of blue, or gray, or any other color that is also so overly represented in our growing yarn stash?*

But even though I have my favorites, one of my greatest joys in handcrafting is the discovery of something new. A fabric line from a new artist, or the first sewing pattern from a beginning pattern designer, or a brand new yarn from a yarn dyer who's trying something a little different. I love that feeling of discovery I get when I find something that or someone who is new to me.

Getting to meet so many hand crafters who are not in the national spotlight has led me to think quite a bit about why and how particular makers and artists become well-known in this new age of social media, Ravelry, and online ordering. One of my favorite parts about creating new issues of **By Hand** is the discovery of fiber and fabric artists who have not yet "made it." There are so many makers in the communities I explore who, although talented and accomplished, have not achieved big name recognition.

And why not? It's been my observation that the knitting industry, like so many others, is a tough nut to crack. Once you make it to the inner circle, so to speak, you begin to appear everywhere—on Instagram, as a featured designer in pattern books and collections, at retreats and fiber events, and on podcasts. But this group of industry insiders tends to be very small and insular, and it is often hard for newcomers who don't have these insider connections to find room in the field without name recognition.

My goal since the very first issue of **By Hand** has been to always include some makers whose names aren't already appearing everywhere. When we look for pattern and project designers, I seek out less well-known makers whose beautiful work has not had the opportunity to be seen by a broad audience. I work to include yarn dyers, designers, and other fiber and fabric artists who readers may not have heard of yet. To me, these discoveries are always such a wonderful surprise!

I still love making with my tried-and-true patterns and materials, but I find that more and more, I work to give newcomers a try, as well. I hope that **By Hand** encourages you as makers to spread your wings a little bit, too. Try a new project or even a new type of hand crafting. Knit or sew a pattern from a designer you aren't familiar with. Take a chance on a yarn you've not heard of or knit with before. By supporting these makers, we all help to encourage a wider field in the fiber and fabric industry, and to give more people a chance to live their passion and to bring us along on their voyage.

Warmly,

Andrea

Tolt Yarn and Wool is one of the most beautiful yarn stores I have ever had the pleasure of visiting. Although the entry is unassuming, the artful displays in the large front windows hint at the store's sense of style. Stepping through the door, you notice immediately the special touches that make the store so visually appealing: large rustic wooden cabinets with yarns arrayed in rainbows of color, soaring ceilings, wood block tables that I long to have in my own home, where yarn is splayed out in displays that make your fingers itch to touch the skeins. Everything is well-organized and in its place, yet the effect is one of plenitude and yarny lushness.

My awe at the beauty of the store morphs into yarn-lover's delight as I browse through the displays and find all the yarns that I love: Brooklyn Tweed, Woolfolk, YOTH, Quince & Co, Imperial, Jamieson, Cestari, and Heirloom Romney, just to name a few. Equally exciting are the new-to-me local and regional yarns that I've never gotten to meet before, such as Thirteen Mile, Hinterland, Elemental Affects, and Insouciant Fibers.

It is clear in every inch of the store that the person who started it all truly and deeply loves yarn. This impression is confirmed when I meet Anna Dianich. She is exactly the type of yarn owner you hope to find in your own LYS: cheerful, kind, welcoming, and deeply enthusiastic about all things fiber-related. Anna and her husband recently bought 80 acres nearby on which to build a home for themselves, their four children, and their collection of animals, including chickens, goats, sheep, a horse and a donkey, dogs and cats.

Anna's decision to open a yarn store in the small town of Carnation grew out of her desire to create community. "I had this great group of ladies I was meeting with, and living out here, there wasn't a close yarn shop, and I thought this town needed a place for people to gather." Anna explains that although she had no business experience, when the space became available, she bought the building. Her husband, who is a skilled builder and remodeler, helped create the environment she envisioned.

Anna says that the decision to carry particular yarn lines evolved organically. "I love hardy wool with a story behind it, particularly from domestic ranchers, or based in traditional knitting from Europe." Anna's innate sense for unique and special yarns—including brands that aren't already well-known—has given Tolt a reputation far beyond its small-town setting. Anna has built not only a loyal local following, but a fan base around the country that shops online and visits Tolt as a knitter's destination, as well.

In the almost four years since its opening, Tolt has created several annual events that have inspired knitters near and far. Every March, the store hosts Icelandic Wool Month, which grew out of Anna's trip to Iceland. The event has created a new audience for Lettopi, a traditional Icelandic wool that is featured in a special colorwork sweater design created just for the event each year. And every summer, Tolt hosts Camp Tolt. "I love to hike and camp, to knit outside and to knit garments that are hardy and durable," Anna explains. Camp Tolt invites knitters to come together and knit in the local park on the banks of the Tolt River. Special patterns and swag are part of the summer-long event.

In 2015, Anna published *Farm to Needle: Stories of Wool*. "It was so much fun to put together because we got to travel, take photos, and meet yarn and fiber producers," she recalls. "But it was scary, too, because we had a really short deadline, and I had never done anything like this before." The Introduction in *Farm to Needle* explains that the ethos "simply means knowing where your yarn came from and who helped it get to you along the way . . . Feeling connected with the origins of our yarn increases the satisfaction and joy we experience with our projects." This desire to connect with sheep farmers and wool producers also led to Anna's decision to create her own yarn line: Snoqualmie Valley Yarn (you can read about this yarn's remarkable origin story on the following pages).

Anna emphasizes that Tolt has been a group effort from the very beginning, and she credits her family and her employees with the store's growth and success. The number and variety of classes offered year-round, the events and periodic makers' markets hosted there, and the friendly and welcoming atmosphere of the store all realize Anna's vision of using yarn and knitting to build community. ⌘

Tolt Yarn and Wool

Owner: Anna Dianach

Website: toltyarnandwool.com

Address: 4509 Tolt Ave., Carnation

Phone: 425.333.4066

Farm to Needle: Snoqualmie Valley Yarn

Snoqualmie Valley Yarn began with Anna Dianich's daily commute to work: driving through farmland and fields, she noticed a flock of sheep that she passed each day. Curious, she stopped one day to talk to farmer Jeff Rogers, who along with his wife Katya, owns three farms that comprise Snoqualmie Valley Lamb. This initial conversation led to a business partnership and a lasting friendship between two people who shared a common passion.

Jeff has worked for years on the genetics of both sheep and grass in order to create a sustainable, organic system. His process emphasizes stewardship of the land, and it is clear that he cares deeply for both the animals he works with and the land he farms. Jeff breeds Clun Forest and Blue Faced Leicester (BFL), and then cross breeds the two, and it is the wool of this cross breed that is used to create Snoqualmie Valley Yarn. The lambs are bred for meat, but until Anna came along, Jeff had little to no use for the wool produced from each shearing.

The yarn that resulted from Jeff and Anna's partnership embodies the concept of "farm to needle," and is featured in Anna's book of the same name. Snoqualmie Valley Yarn is available in-store and online at Tolt Yarn and Wool. ⌘

When we visited the Snoqualmie Valley sheep, we were lucky enough to get to see mamas and their babies together, including these three-day-old lambs (above and to the left).

You can view Snoqualmie Falls from a lookout at the top, or walk the one-mile
path to the base. Or, hike one of the many trails in the surrounding state park
through dense forests carpeted with ferns and moss.

Hand Stitched Memories
by Andrea Hungerford

These beautiful embroidery patterns were designed by talented illustrator Peggy Dean, who also creates the maps at the beginning of the **By Hand** serials. The first is a drawing of found botanicals, inspired by a hike through field and forest. I love this sketch because it evokes the beauty of simple native plants that surround us every day and often go unnoticed until you stop to take time to admire the little details.

The second is a willow tree, designed to grace the cover of a "family tree" book— one that records genealogy, family lore, stories and memories that make up your heritage. I love the graceful lines of the willow, and it brings to mind summer days that I spend sitting under a similar tree in our backyard, kept cool by the long hanging branches.

In creating an embroidery design, I strove to keep the stitches simple, so that even a maker just learning to embroider would be able to master this project.

Stitches used for the willow tree: Back stitch (trunk) and lazy daisy doubled (for the leaves).

Stitches used for the found botanicals: Back stitch, lazy daisy, French knot, chain stitch, and cross stitch.

One of the wonderful things about this project is that you can make it your own through your choice of color palettes. The following are some of the DMC embroidery floss colors that I used: 154. 223, 472, 758, 801, 902, 937, 3012, 3345, 3346, 3350, 3773, 3802, 3803, 3866.

Instead of trying to trace the patterns onto fabric, I used Sulky Sticky Fabri-Solvy, which makes it all so much easier! Simply print the pattern out on the Sulky paper (you can download the designs on your computer by going to byhandserial/squarespace.com/patterns), then peel off the backing, stick the Sulky paper to your fabric, and begin stitching. You won't need an embroidery hoop, because the Sulky paper makes the fabric stiff enough on its own. When your embroidery is complete, rinse the fabric under warm water and the paper dissolves, leaving only your lovely stitches.

Embroidery is particularly beautiful when it decorates the cover of a book: a photo album, garden journal, personal diary, or even a record of your daily "to do" lists. I made these covers from Warsa Linen in color Ecru (available in-store or online at Purl Soho) to fit an 8"x10" book (which actually has a cover sized 8.25" x 11").

SEWING INSTRUCTIONS

1. Cut a piece of Warsa Linen 14" x 25".

2. Fold it onto the book you'll be covering so that you can eyeball where you want the design placed. Then adhere the design to the linen in the chosen location, and embroider.

3. When embroidery is complete, trim the fabric to a final size of 13" wide x 23.5" long (this gives you a chance to even out any sides that have gotten wonky while you were embroidering).

4. Fold the two long edges inward, toward the wrong side, by ½" and press. Then fold over ½" again and press again. Sew these two hems in place (before you sew the second hem, hold the fabric up to your book and see if you want to create a slightly larger or smaller hem so that it exactly matches the edges of your book).

5. Fold the two short edges inward, toward the wrong side, by ¼" and press, then fold over ¼" again and press again. Sew these two hems in place.

6. Fold in the two hemmed short edges by 2.75" and press (again, check against your book to see if you've achieved a proper fit). Hand sew the top and bottom sides of each edge in place, using a slip stitch. I did this while fitting the cover around the book, so that I could achieve a perfect fit.

Your book cover should be removable but fit snugly when in place. ⌘

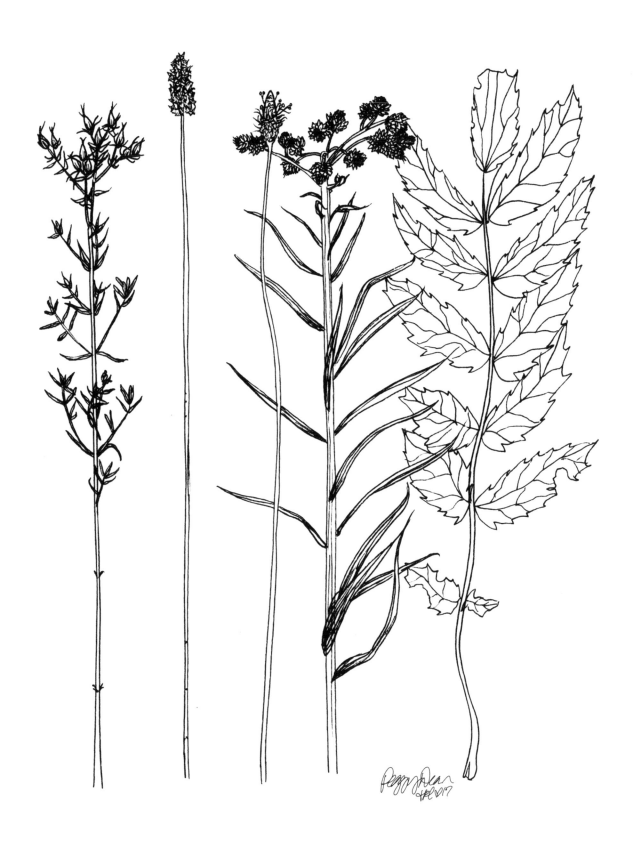

Breathtaking sunsets over Bellingham Bay and the overwater walkway leading to Boulevard Park.

Vibrant Color: Hazel Knits

There's a lot of activity at Hazel Knits these days, as the business reaches its tenth anniversary and moves into new headquarters. The new location—with lots of natural light, tall windows and ceilings, and plenty of room—will house the entire dyeing operation, with space for a drying room, storage, an office, and retail space as well. Dyers Wendee Shulsen and Dave Decoteau are thrilled to finally be able to move their yarn dyeing business out of their home: "Until now, we've had the skeiners in the bedroom, yarn stacked in the driveway under tarps, and so many boxes in the living room that we haven't seen our couch for a year!" says Wendee. "Dave has had to dye outside in lobster cooking pots on propane burners, in all seasons, during rain, and snow, and summer heat. Sometimes he would be dyeing at night, in the dark and the rain, with only a head lamp for lighting." The Hazel Knits duo looked for a space for two years until they found a location that provided for sufficient power and water, and a reasonable rental rate —not easy to find in the Seattle area. When they found the building, Dave says that "it was a disaster... covered in graffiti, in unusable condition. It was a leap of faith, but the owner took the building down to the studs and completely rebuilt it."

These days, the building looks brand new, and it houses an artists' community of painters, a sculptor, a dance studio, and ginger beer makers. Dave and Wendee can utilize up to 12 dye pots at a time. Their dyeing process involves a great deal of artistry and color sense. Wendee explains: "We measure everything by weight and milliliter, and we use only ten colors of dye. That includes black and three browns. I think that having so few colors to work with takes more creativity, but it also makes the yarn line more cohesive. When you buy pre-mixed dye, there are a lot of purifiers and fillers. For us, the dye is as saturated as can be. It's dye in a pretty pure color form, and then we create all of the other colors ourselves by mixing." While Wendee is the visionary for color, Dave is the master of the dyeing process. "It's definitely been a learning curve," he says. "Color is extremely temperamental. PH, temperature, duration of temperature all affect how it comes out in the end. Every color has its own personality and reacts differently to minute changes."

Wendee started Hazel Knits back when she was working at a yarn store in the area and noticed that the few indie dyers who existed at the time were in high demand. "I saw this niche that needed filling. People were asking for these hand dyed yarns every day, and I thought I'd try it, even though I'd never dyed yarn before." Wendee taught herself, through a lot of research and a great deal of trial and error. At the time, there were also very few yarn suppliers, and it was difficult to get a mill to do a custom spun yarn line, but creating her own yarn was very important to Wendee. "I bought a ton of yarn and dyed it up, did a lot of comparing. Then when I finally found a mill in Canada, we sent samples with customized fibers and weights back and forth until finally we got it right. That first line became our Artisan Sock, which we still sell today. My first order was 500 pounds, and it was one of those 'deep breath' moments. At that time, I was still dyeing in my basement, using electric turkey roasters and a hand cranked skeiner."

Slowly but surely, Wendee invested in new equipment and started introducing new lines. Currently, Hazel Knits sells ten bases, from lace all the way up to super bulky, in a variety of fibers, including merino, cashmere, silk, and nylon. Next up will be yarn lines spun from plant fibers. Dave started helping Wendee dye about seven years ago, and eventually joined her business full-time.

Hazel Knits is sold online, at local yarn shows and trunk shows, and through select retail yarn stores. Next steps include opening a retail space in the new building, and adding employees. Dave and Wendee hope to build a more manageable schedule that allows for a little more work-life balance.

During the ten years that Wendee has been dyeing, she has seen a lot of changes in the knitting world. "When I first started dyeing, everyone wanted variegated yarn …Then Ravelry comes along and all of a sudden you have all of these patterns, and knitters are getting better and you're knitting more for the pattern. This is what defines my palette and the way I dye. I want people to be able to knit complicated things and be able to see their stitches. I want my handiwork to be the starting point for their finished handiwork." Hazel Knits' focus on beautiful, saturated colors and tonal dyeing creates a stunning palette that is beautiful in its own right, but also allows a knitter's own work—be it shape, or texture, or stitch pattern—to shine through. ⌘

Hazel Knits

Color Creationists: Wendee Shulsen and Dave Decoteau

Website: hazelknits.com

Instagram: hazelknits and hazelknitsdave

Puget Sound Shawl

By Michele Lee Bernstein

FINISHED MEASUREMENTS
Wingspan 54"
Depth 27"

MATERIALS
Hazel Knits Entice (70% superwash merino/20% cashmere/10% nylon, 400 yards per 113 g)
Colors: MC 1 skein in Hoppy Blonde (yellow) and CC 1 skein in Splish Splash (blue) [pictured above]
MC 1 skein Twilight (dark blue) and CC 1 skein Frost (light blue) [pictured on following pages]

US 4 (3.5 mm) 32" circular needle
Cable needle (cn), tapestry needle, stitch markers

GAUGE
23 sts = 4" in stockinette stitch (St st), unblocked

NOTES

This is a half-circle pi shawl, worked flat. The various "rings" incorporate lace, stripes, and slipped-stitch color work. Gauge is not critical for this pattern, but if your gauge is significantly different you may require more or less yarn than specified.

DIRECTIONS

Garter Tab

With MC, CO 3 sts. Knit 6 rows.

Next row (RS): K3, rotate work 90° and pick up and knit 3 sts along side edge, rotate 90° again and pick up and knit 3 sts from CO edge. 9 sts.

Next row: K3, pm, p3, pm, k3.

This 9 stitch "garter tab" is the beginning of your shawl. The first and last 3 sts of each row form the edging, and are worked in garter stitch throughout (knit every row). The body of the shawl grows from the 3 center sts.

Sun Half-Circle

Row 1 (RS): K3, sl m, yo, kfb, yo, k1, yo, kfb, yo, sl m, k3. 15 sts.

Row 2: K3, sl m, purl to last 3 sts, sl m, k3.

Row 3: Knit.

Row 4: Rep Row 2.

Row 5 (RS): K3, sl m, *k1, yo; rep from * to last 3 sts, sl m, k3. 24 sts.

Rows 6-12: Maintaining the 3 sts in garter at each edge, work in St st beg with a purl row for 7 rows.

Row 13 (RS): K3, sl m, *k1, yo; rep from * to last 3 sts, sl m, k3. 42 sts.

Rows 14-28: Maintaining the 3 sts in garter at each edge, work in St st beg with a purl row for 15 rows.

Row 29 (RS): K3, sl m, *k1, yo; rep from * to last 3 sts, sl m, k3. 78 sts.

Rows 30-44: Maintaining the 3 sts in garter at each edge, work in St st beg with a purl row for 15 rows.

Row 45 (RS): K3, sl m, *k2tog, yo; rep from * to last 3 sts, sl m, k3.

Rows 46-60: Maintaining the 3 sts in garter at each edge, work in St st beg with a purl row for 15 rows.

Row 61 (RS): K3, sl m, *yo, k1; rep from * to last 3 sts, sl m, k3. 150 sts.

Rows 62-64: Maintaining the 3 sts in garter at each edge, work in St st beg with a purl row for 3 rows.

Sun Stripes

Join CC. Do not cut yarns when changing colors, but carry the unused color up the side of the work.

Row 1 (RS): With CC, k3, sl m, k3, *sl 2 pwise wyib, k15; rep from * to last 8 sts, sl 2 pwise wyib, k3, sl m, k3.

Row 2: With CC, k3, sl m, p3, *sl 2 pwise wyif, p15; rep from * to last 8 sts, sl 2 pwise wyif, p3, sl m, k3.

Row 3: With MC, knit.

Row 4: With MC, k3, sl m, purl to last 3 sts, sl m, k3.

Rows 5-28: Rep Rows 1-4 six more times.

Row 29 (RS): With CC, k3, sl m, k3, *sl 2 pwise wyib, k32; rep from * to last 8 sts, sl 2 pwise wyib, k3, sl m, k3.

Row 30: With CC, k3, sl m, p3, *sl 2 pwise wyif, p32; rep from * to last 8 sts, sl 2 pwise wyif, p3, sl m, k3.

Row 31: With MC, knit.

Row 32: With MC, k3, sl m, purl to last 3 sts, sl m, k3.

Rows 33-56: Rep Rows 29-32 six more times.

Rainy Sky

Cut MC and continue with CC only.

Row 1 (RS): K3, sl m, *k1, yo; rep from * to last 3 sts, sl m, k3. 294 sts.

Maintaining the 3 sts in garter at each edge, work in St st beg with a purl row for 5 rows.

Work Rows 1-18 of Rainy Sky chart.

Maintaining the 3 sts in garter at each edge, work in St st beg with a knit row for 4 rows.

Seagulls 1

Note: It is important to keep the carried strand loose because of the stretch needed when blocking. After slipping stitches, spread them out on right needle before knitting next stitch.

Join MC. Do not cut yarns when changing colors, but carry the unused color up the side of the work.

Row 1 (RS): With MC, k3, sl m, k4, *sl 5 pwise wyif, k5; rep from * to last 7 sts, k4, sl m, k3.

Row 2: With MC, k3, sl m, p4, *p5, sl 5 pwise wyif; rep from * to last 7 sts, p4, sl m, k3.

Row 3: With CC, k3, sl m, k4, *k5, sl 5 pwise wyif; rep from * to last 7 sts, k4, sl m, k3.

Row 4: With CC, k3, sl m, p4, *sl 5 pwise wyif, p5; rep from * to last 7 sts, p4, sl m, k3.

Row 5: With MC, k3, sl m, k4, *sl 2 pwise wyib, use right needle to pick up MC strand from 4 rows below and knit it together with next st, sl 2 pwise wyib, k5; rep from * to last 7 sts, k4, sl m, k3.

Row 6: With MC, k3, sl m, p4, *p5, sl 2 pwise wyif, p1, sl 2 pwise wyif; rep from * to last 7 sts, p4, sl m, k3.

Row 7: With CC, k3, sl m, k4, *k5, sl 2 pwise wyib, pick up CC strand from 4 rows below and knit it tog with next st, sl 2 pwise wyib; rep from * to last 7 sts, k4, sl m, k3.

Row 8: With CC, k3, sl m, p4, *sl 2 pwise wyif, p1, sl 2 pwise wyif, p5; rep from * to last 7 sts, p4, sl m, k3.

Olympic Mountains

Cut CC and continue with MC only.

Row 1 (RS): Knit to last 4 sts, kfb, sl m, k3. 295 sts.

Maintaining the 3 sts in garter at each edge, work in St st beg with a purl row for 5 rows.

Work Rows 1-16 of Olympic Mountains chart. We recommend placing markers between pattern repeats on the first row.

Next row (RS): Knit to last 5 sts, k2tog, sl m, k3. 294 sts.

Maintaining the 3 sts in garter at each edge, work in St st beg with a purl row for 3 rows.

Seagulls II
Join CC. Do not cut yarns when changing colors, but carry the unused color up the side of the work.
Work same as Seagulls I, but with colors inverted (work Rows 1-2 and 5-6 with CC, Rows 3-4 and 7-8 with MC).

Waves
Cut MC and continue with CC only.
Row 1 (RS): Knit to last 4 sts, kfb, sl m, k3. 295 sts.
Row 2: K3, sl m, purl to last 3 sts, sl m, k3.
Work Rows 1-6 of Waves chart 3 times, then work Rows 1-4 of chart once. We recommend placing markers between pattern repeats on the first row.

Edging and Bind Off
Cut CC.
With MC, knit 2 rows.
BO all sts with MC as follows: K2, *insert left needle into fronts of 2 sts on right needle and knit them together through the back loop, k1; rep from * until 1 st remains. Cut yarn and draw through last loop.

FINISHING
Wet block to half circle shape, pinning out scallops at increase points along edging. Weave in and trim all ends.

Rainy Sky

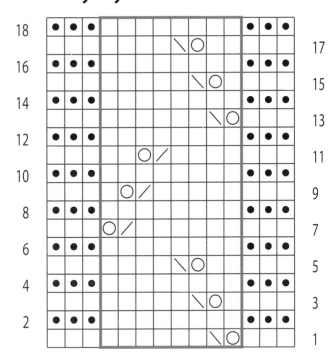

Waves

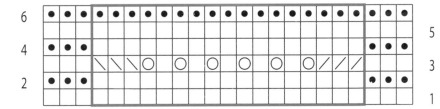

Olympic Mountains

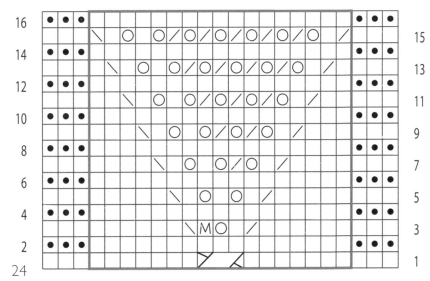

24

ABBREVIATIONS

BO – bind off, bound-off

CC - contrast color

K – knit

K2tog – knit 2 sts together

MC – main color

M1 – make 1: with right needle, pick up running thread between needles from back to front and place it on left needle, then knit it through the back loop

P – purl

P2tog – purl 2 sts together

Rem – remain

RS – right side

Ssk – [sl 1 as if to knit] 2 times, insert left needle into these 2 sts and knit them together

St(s) – stitch(es)

WS – wrong side

Wyif – with yarn in front

Cn - cable needle

CO - cast on, cast-on

Kfb – increase 1 st by knitting into front, then back of same st

M – marker

Pm – place marker

Pwise – purlwise/as if to purl

Rep – repeat

Sl - slip

St st – stockinette stitch

Wyib – with yarn in back

Yo – yarn over

Water surrounds you in the Puget Sound region, whether you're at the ferry dock on Bainbridge Island (above) or watching the sun set over Sarasota Passage on Whidbey Island (below).

Hand Poured: Wax & Wool Etc.

Kjerste Whaley's creation of Wax & Wool Etc's signature candles epitomizes the care and craft that goes into making by hand. Kjerste's work space is immaculate: compact but well-supplied, with everything in its place. It is dominated by "Big Bertha," the oversized wax melter that gleams in the corner. Kjerste explains that she fills Big Bertha with wax (which arrives in flake form) around dinner time, turns "her" on, and then heats the studio, as well, to reach an optimal pouring temperature, as the ambient air temperature will effect how the wax pours and sets. "By the time the kids are in bed, the wax is hot and the studio is ready." She pours the candles in small batches of eight jars, first measuring out the wax by weight and adding essential oils. The wax has to reach a specific temperature before it is poured, and Kjerste pours into hot jars, to keep the wax from separating away from the sides of the jars as it cools. The wax is poured (after wicks are fixed in the empty jars), the wicks are centered, the jars are spaced for cooling, and the next day, Kjerste trims the wicks and affixes the labels. She hand labels the scent on each candle label in her neat handwriting, which adds the final handmade touch.

To watch Kjerste's slow and steady work, you wouldn't guess that she is also the mother to five children, all under the age of ten (including three-year-old twins). Yet it's the very demands of mothering that make the creative process such an important outlet for Kjerste. "I love having a product I can point to at the end of the day that I made. I love the natural rhythm of my work. I lose myself in the process—the warmth of the studio, the scent of the candles, the quiet solitude while I work. No matter how tired I am at the end of a day of parenting, when the kids are in bed and I head out to my studio, I feel like I get a fresh start." Kjerste's creative work is rooted in her upbringing: she was one of eight children, and many of her family members worked with their hands, including her mother, who grew and canned her own food, sewed, knit, embroidered, and smocked. "I was raised by people whose hands were never idle. They lived simply and seasonally. I love that."

27

Kjerste's own family is also part of the foundation of her creative business; she speaks of the importance of the support her husband gives to her work, and the assistance of her sister (who has done all of the photography for Wax & Wool Etc's website and marketing). The value of creative hand work permeates her household, as evidenced by her nine-year-old daughter's recent foray into handcrafted bar soaps as a small business of her own after reading a "how-to" book from the library. Kjerste says, "I think it's good for them to see us actively involved in growing something and being industrious. We're leading by example and growing the next generation of makers and entrepreneurs."

Kjerste began hand pouring candles after seeing some at a local farmer's market. A hobby that first generated gifts for family and friends morphed into selling at a holiday craft bazaar, then a shop on Etsy, and now includes sales through over 20 retailers such as Twig & Horn in Maine, My Sister Knits in Colorado, and Never Not Knitting in California.

Part of what makes Wax & Wool Etc's candles unique are the scents that Kjerste develops. Fresh linen, coconut lime, evergreen state, and herb garden are just a few. She recently worked with a northwestern yarn store and a cupcake bakery to create signature scents. Wax & Wool Etc. also offers a line of "gentlemen's reserve" candles in scents such as bourbon, tobacco, and leather. Kjerste laughingly reports that she is resisting others' efforts to get her to nickname the product line "mandles."

Wax & Wool Etc. got its name because Kjerste has always sold both candles and knitted items; she says that she is an "obsessive" knitter, although she also sews and weaves. "We threw an 'etc.' in our name so we wouldn't feel completely tied down to one thing. I am passionate about trying new things and from time to time those things make their way into the shop." For instance, Wax & Wool Etc. carries "Busy Happy Hands," hand salves that Kjerste explains are perfect for knitters' hands.

As is the case for many makers, Kjerste finds it difficult at times to balance work and family, and to grow a small business from the ground up. "I think as a handcrafter it can also be difficult to be taken seriously as a business … but then there's always the joy of doing what I love that pulls me back. My work is meaningful. It brings me pleasure and beautifies my life and the lives of others." ⌘

Wax & Wool Etc.

Creator: Kjerste Whaley

Website: etsy.com/shop/waxand-wooletc

Instagram: waxandwool

Products: Small batch hand poured soy candles, lip balms, hand salves, knitting and notions bags

Homegrown: Local Color Fiber Studio

Local Color Fiber Studio is truly a farm to needle operation. Emily Tseng raises fiber animals, farms local dye plants, has her fiber locally milled, and then dyes her yarn with the natural dyes derived from the plants she's harvested. She accomplishes all of this labor-intensive work almost single-handedly on picturesque Bainbridge Island.

Emily's foray into yarn production started with owning angora rabbits, and then Finn sheep when they were offered to her by a fellow islander who was looking to retire. The Finns are small statured and compact, with a wide variety of colorful fleece. They are friendly by nature, and they clearly know Emily and look forward to her visits to the pasture, crowding around her to be petted when she steps through the gate. Emily has her fiber milled at Abundant Earth Fiber Mill on Whidbey Island; one of the resulting yarns is Whole Flock, comprised of 80% Finn wool and 20% angora. She purchases additional domestically raised yarn from mills in Wyoming and New York for yarn dyeing, as well.

Next came the dye plants; Emily has a background in vegetable farming, and while she was apprenticing on a farm property, she decided to experiment with growing dye plants. Although she was already a knitter, she had no experience dyeing. "I had a background in the farm-to-table local food scene, and I wanted to apply those ideals to yarn," she explains.

The dye plants are raised on an acre of land made available to Emily by Bainbridge Vineyards, where she also works. The winery and vineyards, which sit on forty acres, make up the longest continually operating farm in the county. The Suyematu family was the original owner, and they logged the farm with horses in the 1920s. Because they were Japanese-Americans, they were interned during World War II, but returned to the land and continued to grow berries (as did most of the farmers on the island, making it the strawberry capitol of the Northwest) until they sold the property in 1982. The

vineyard has occupied the land for over thirty years now as an operating winery, vineyard, and grower of raspberries and pumpkins.

Emily grows a wide variety of plants to use for dyeing, including coreopsis, marigold, cabbage, indigo, dahlias, and sunflowers (the seeds are used for dyeing). "It's hard to know how much to grow, because I'm limited by how much I can harvest," Emily explains. So she does a lot of staggered plantings to extend the harvest time. All of the dye plants are annuals except for the dahlias, whose tubers must be dug up in the fall and replanted every spring.

After the plants are harvested, Emily creates the dye. "Most plants, you create a dye by making them into a kind of a tea and using the water," she explains. "Indigo is different, because it isn't water soluble. You harvest the leaves in bundles, then weigh them down in stock tanks of warm water. After a week or so, you oxygenate the water, take out the plants, then slough off the water, and the leftover sludge is what you use to dye." Emily also uses foraged plants, such as nettles and sumac, and leftover plant materials, such as onion skins and grape skins discarded by the winery.

Local Color Fiber Studio yarns are sold online and through several yarn shops, including Churchmouse Yarn and Teas and Tolt Yarn and Wool, where Emily recently collaborated with Anna Dianich to custom-dye Snoqualmie Valley Yarn. Emily has also begun traveling to local and regional shows, including Black Sheep, Madrona, and Knit City. Yarns available including fingering, DK, and worsted weight. In addition, Emily has begun natural dye and indigo dye workshops at the winery, where participants get to harvest their own dye plants, create their own dye, and then dye up their own skeins of yarn.

There are many challenges to this labor-intensive process of bringing local, naturally dyed yarns to knitters, including "educating people what the product is like," says Emily. "Naturally dyed can be inconsistent from batch to batch, so you have to embrace the unique beauty of each individual skein." Also, the price point is higher. "What you're paying for is someone growing an agricultural product, versus synthetic dyes from large chemical corporations." Emily contrasts the method used by vegetable CSAs, which allow you to collect money up front through subscriptions purchased for the growing season and then budget what you have to spend for the year, with the agricultural process she uses, which requires spending money first to create the yarn and then hoping that you can recoup your sunk costs through subsequent yarn sales.

Up to now, Emily has been raising animals and dye plants on leased properties around Bainbridge Island, but she and her husband have recently purchased eleven acres of bare land along the Puyullup River. They've planted five acres as pasture for the Finn sheep, and they're enrolling the acreage along the river in a USDA program for water quality, which means they will agree not to farm up to the river's edge, but instead do native plantings. The next steps are septic, irrigation, power, and eventually a house and barn, and the remaining acreage will be used for dye plants.

It is both inspiring and overwhelming to visit the pastures and fields with Emily and understand the scope of work that she accomplishes, truly "by hand," in order to realize the ethos of local, organic, farm-to-needle yarn for her customers. It gives new meaning to the yarn I hold in my hands when I pick up a skein of Local Color Fiber Studio yarn. When you understand all that has transpired in order to bring that yarn to your needles, it infuses your own work with more care and meaning. In this way, the work and skill of local farms truly is brought to the knitter's needles. ⌘

Local Color Fiber Studio

Farmer, shepherd and dyer: Emily Tzeng

Website: localcolorfiberstudio.squarespace.com

Instagram: localcolorfiberstudio

Yarns: In-house yarn lines from Finn sheep and angora rabbits, and naturallly dyed yarns from farmed and foraged dye plants and materials

Day Trip: Bainbridge Island

Bainbridge Shops and Eateries

Walk along Winslow Street in the center of town, just a ten-minute stroll from the ferry, and be sure to stop to eat and shop at:

* Streamliner Diner
* Churchmouse Yarns & Teas
* Eagle Harbor Books
* Petit & Olsen
* Blackbird Bakery
* Mora Ice Creamery
* Salt House Mercantile
* Bon Bon Confections

In just a few minutes more, you can walk down to the waterfront and find:
* Docs Marina Grill
* Pegasus Coffee

Bainbridge Points of Interest

From the ferry ride to the waterfront to the forested trails, you will find the natural beauty of the Island's flora and fauna, including bald eagles, sea lions and seals, and the iconic banana slug. Take time to visit:
* Islandwood Environmental Education Center
* Bainbridge Vineyards
* Boedel Reserve
* Bainbridge Art Museum

ICE CREAMS & SORBE

7

Bainbridge Island's Churchmouse Yarns & Teas

When Kit Hutchin wrote a business plan over seventeen years ago, the first line read: "Churchmouse Yarns & Teas will be a place of community . . ." According to Kit and her husband and co-owner John Koval, "today, that mission still drives what we do—in the store, with our pattern publishing, and online with our widely extended audience."

For many, Churchmouse needs no introduction; it is widely considered to be one of the preeminent destination yarn store in the country. Inside, you will find a map with hundreds of red pins identifying visitors' home towns all over the world. The store itself is expertly stocked, wide open and welcoming, and staffed by some of the most friendly knitting experts you'll ever meet. To add to the ambiance, Churchmouse is located on Bainbridge Island. Only a 35-minute relaxing and scenic ferry ride from Seattle, visiting the island is like entering another world. The stroll from the ferry down Winslow Street invites visitors to stop in coffee shops, eateries, a bookstore, art galleries, and one of the best ice creameries found anywhere in the world.

Before opening the store, Kit spent so much time volunteering at her local church and teaching knitting classes there that John nicknamed her "the churchmouse." John says, "the name popped into her head when she noticed a tiny ceramic mouse peering out of a teacup on her kitchen counter. No other name was even considered." John explains that the "& Teas" part of the name "suggests other ways you can add beauty and comfort to your crafting, such as knitting with a hearty cuppa poured from a traditional Brown Betty teapot into a handmade English mug with a bit of Scottish shortbread."

When asked to explain Churchmouse's national prominence, John says: "For seventeen years at Churchmouse, we've pedaled as fast as we can, remaining absolutely dedicated to providing an outstanding customer experience at every point of contact, in person and online—every customer, every time. It took us seventeen years to become an overnight success." He goes on to note that two decisions have moved Churchmouse forward: First, publication of the Churchmouse Classics patterns. Since 2009, over 100 original Churchmouse Classics patterns have

been published, and are now carried in nearly 700 yarn stores around the world. Second, "after literally years of concept work," Churchmouse launched its online store, referred to in-house as "Churchmouse Yarns dot calm." John says that "Kit really wanted to create a personalized experience in digital format that matched her vision of the store (a welcoming place of community with a residential feel)."

Kit's official title is owner, founder, and chief executive officer, with a particular focus on brand and vision —"arbiter of the brand," as John puts it. John calls himself the "customer experience director," and the chief merchandising officer is Pam White. Kit emphasizes that running the store is a team effort, relying on the talents of all 30 of the full and part-time employees.

Churchmouse stocks both well-known yarns such as Rowan, Berroco, and Brooklyn Tweed, and small batches of local yarns, such as Local Color Fiber Studio and Insouciant Fibers. The Plucky Knitter has created color palettes with Churchmouse names exclusively for the store, which often sell out within minutes.

But it is not just the fine selection of yarns that sets Churchmouse apart.

You will find dozens of sample knits throughout the store that inform and inspire, as well as a carefully curated collection of tools and notions. The teas section of the store is both beautiful and calming, making you feel as if you really could sit in the small courtyard outside Churchmouse's front door and relax with a cuppa. Here you will find an extensive variety of teas, pots, and mugs, including Church-mouse-branded teas from Steven Smith of Portland. Their "Summer" tea, for example, is like a lovely gift, each bag looking more like a silk sachet of flowers than a standard tea bag. Also throughout the store are beautiful "lifestyle" pleasures such as classic eyeglass readers from Paris, Blackwing Pencils, and notebooks and journals, project boxes, and enameled brass tags all made exclusively for Churchmouse.

To add to all of this, the store also offers a long list of classes and knitting groups throughout the year, and has hosted two Knitting With Company retreats. Starting this fall, Churchmouse will host its own knitting retreat at Islandwood, a beautiful outdoor learning center set in 250 acres of forest only a few minutes' drive from the store.

Kit's long history in the knitting industry places her in a unique position to recognize trends in both knitting and in the expansion of the knitting community. "I think that people are becoming more interested in developing their craft, getting a little deeper. They want to expand their skills, not just buy stash yarn. Our focus is on helping knitters have success, choose the right project, develop skills as they go, finish it beautifully, and wear it until it's worn out." Kit notes how knitters are inspired to seek out community, and how it can be the basis for forming friendships. "It's an immediate shared experience."

After so many years, Kit says that it's the people, first and foremost, that keep her loving what she does. "And then yarn. I still get a thrill, walking through the shelves." In reflecting on the company's growth and development, John explains that "one key core value that . . . will never change is Kit's focus on helping her customers be successful with their knitting, crocheting, and stitching. Churchmouse can be considered a 'project shop' rather than a 'yarn shop.' Customers come here to find a project they can finish, enjoy making, and love wearing, not just more yarn to stash." ⌘

Ferry Crossing Quilt

by Andrea Hungerford

My inspirations for this quilt were the Washington forests, the waters of the Puget Sound, and the magnificent presence of Mt. Rainier towering over it all. Both the joy and the challenge of this quilt is that there are no rules and no pattern. Your imagination and creativity are all that you need!

This project is a great stashbuster. You can use virtually any fabric that inspires you. Try small print florals, or batiks, or a collection of solids. In order to achieve the effect I was looking for, I wanted to use a very special fabric: hand dyed silk hemp. Each piece of this fabric is individually dyed by Jackson Fabric Arts, who describe the silk hemp as "a cross weave fabric, with silk and hemp fibers being interwoven. The hemp contributes great strength and durability to the fabric and makes it easy to care for. Silk gives it a soft and fluid drape and a slight sheen . . . silk hemp is easy to hand stitch like silk, but has the added bonus of hemp. Hemp contributes durability and strength to this fabric."

I used a variety of blues, greens, and purples, with a small piece of yellow-gold in the sunset. Each color was cut from a 9"x28" piece, except for both the light and dark amethyst purples and the undyed white, all of which required 18"x28" pieces. I washed all of the fabrics prior to beginning my cuts.

To begin, I determined the finished size I desired, and the approximate order of the colors I wanted to use. For the water, I wanted the colors to start with deep water dark blues and slowly transition to pale blue and turquoise to represent the surface waters. For the forests, I mixed the greens to create the look of layers of dark and light in the forest. And, for the sky, I transitioning from light to dark purples, with streaks of yellow and plum to represent the sky at sunset.

Once I had my order of colors in mind, I simply began cutting. I curved the water and sky fabrics more, to create the impression of waves and clouds, and I cut straighter, narrower pieces for the forest. The mountain is cut from one large piece. I sewed the pieces together as I cut, using ¼" seams. I roughly utilized the rule of thirds: one-third water, one-third forest, and one-third sky.

The ferry is a line drawing, transferred to fabric by printing on iron-on transfer paper. I transferred the drawing to a piece of fabric the same color as the background on which it would be placed, then adhered it with fabric glue until I was ready to more securely tack it in place by quilting around it.

Once the quilt top was complete, I ironed it well and then used remaining undyed fabric for the border, to create the look of a mat around a photograph (my sashing pieces are approximately 4" wide with ½" additional width for seam allowance). Then, I pinned together backing, batting, and top, then began to quilt. I used wavy lines for the water, closely stitched narrow lines for the forest, and open-ended freeform loops in the sky to represent clouds and wind. The mountain is quilted with jagged ridges, one set inside the next, to give the impression of a geological map.

The last step was to bind the quilt; I used a dark gray binding to give the impression of a picture frame. The finished size is 60" x 36".

You can use these same basic principles to create a strip-pieced landscape quilt that embodies any setting or locations: farm or forest, beach or ocean, a field of flowers or a grove of trees in autumn. If you would like to use these beautiful silk hemp fabrics to make your own ferry crossing quilt, you can find a kit with everything you will need for the quilt top available at byhandserial.com. ⌘

46

Local Fabric Store: Drygoods Design

Everything about Drygoods Design is welcoming, from the moment you approach the shop, located in a shady courtyard square and framed with hanging flower baskets. Floor to ceiling windows provide natural light, and high ceilings give the entire space an airy, spacious feeling. But of course, the real treat is what you find inside: beautifully appointed displays with every kind of sewing notion, supply, book, and pattern you could hope for, and a carefully curated selection of 1,500 – 2,000 bolts of fabric. Although Drygoods Design carries all types of fabric—silk, wool, voile, twill, flannel, quilting cotton, etc.—it specializes in woven fabric that is ideally suited for apparel sewing.

The space will soon become even more impressive because, as owner Keli Saw explains, an expansion is in the works. Drygoods Design will soon be taking over the space next door, and plans are in the works for expanded retail space, a knitting classroom, plus a seating area in the new space for makers to gather and work on their projects. Keli tells me that she is hoping to include a wine and tea bar in the new expansion, and eventually an outdoor café, so that makers can sit outside during the summer months. The expansion will provide more room in the main space for classroom instruction, as well as the creation of a pattern room and possibly a weaving classroom upstairs.

Keli's store meets the needs of makers on multiple levels. First, it provides a comprehensive selection of sewing materials and supplies, both online and in-store. "We carry what we love, because if we love it, it's a lot easier for us to find the customers something that they love," Kelly explains. "In some fabric lines, we bring in the whole collection, but for others, it's carefully curated; there's a lot of 'cross-pollinating' between lines, so that we put together the best possible combinations, while offering a wide selection." Apparel fabric lines include Pickering International and Robert Kaufman, and a wide variety

of organic cotton, bamboo, hemp, recycled poly, and Japanese cottons are available. One of Keli's many talents is helping customers select fabrics for apparel sewing: "If you're going to spend all this time to make something, make it something you'd like to wear in three years ... If you buy a good fabric, you'll take more time and care in your work. It's like playing to a strong opponent: you bring your 'A' game."

In addition, Drygoods Design offers four terms of classes each year, most of which sell out. The most popular class is almost always an introduction to sewing, where participants learn not only the basics of sewing, but also how their sewing machines work. Lunch break lessons are also available for professionals working in the neighborhood who want to use their lunchtime to learn something new or work on a project. For more advanced makers, Make it Happen offers "the personal trainers of sewing" to help students work through patterns or projects they've been collecting but haven't managed to work on or finish. "We have a strong apparel sewing community, and we focus not just on construction, but on fit, as well," Keli says. "It's really cool to see the friendships that form in these classes." Up next is a "create-advocate group," that Keli describes as "people who want to have a focal point for activism and advocacy. They can come in and write letters, make quilt blocks to assemble for nonprofit organizations, and find a place where they can feel that they're actually doing something to make a difference."

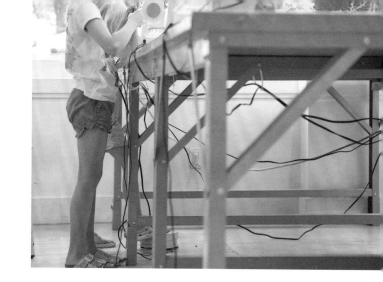

Classes and camps for kids are a part of the lineup, too, including summer sewing camps that sell out almost as soon as they're posted. Keli says, "I think with kids, it's so amazing to see them gain this individual confidence at a young age. It totally propels them further, to understand how long it takes to make something, and what goes into the process. They have this sense of accomplishment, like 'I made this.'"

This combination of beautiful materials to work with, thoughtful instruction on both construction and fit, and the space and time to gather together is what makes Drygoods Design so unique and meaningful for makers. As Keli explains, "people learning from each other is so cool to watch. Making can be such a solitary act, but doing it with others adds meaning and creates community." ⌘

Drygoods Design

Owner: Keli Saw

Website: drygoodsdesignonline.com

Instagram: drygoodsdesign

Address: 301 Occidental Ave. S., Seattle

Phone: 206.535.6950

Farm Fresh:
Pike Place Market

Pike Place Market, located on the Seattle waterfront in the heart of downtown, is a favorite of locals and tourists alike. It was Seattle's original farmers market, established in 1907, and is an open-air market for produce, flowers, seafood, and artisanal foods from local farmers and producers. A recent expansion and plans for further growth promise an even better shopping experience in the years ahead.

Summer blooms at Jello Mold Farm include Alkanet (top), ornamental oregano (middle), Cafe au Lait dahlias (bottom), and the last of the sweet peas (opposite page).

Local Blooms: Jello Mold Farm

Jello Mold Farm is a feast for the senses—lush greenery and brightly colored blooms as far as the eye can see. The smell of growing and flowering plants permeates the air, and the sounds of insects and birds surround you as you walk around the seven acres of farmland in the heart of Skagit Valley. Dennis Westphall and Diane Szukovathy have been selling cut flowers from their farm since 2008, and their expertise is evident from the moment we start to chat.

Both are artists, as showcased by the 1908 farmhouse they call home that is full to bursting with Dennis' stained glass work and a myriad of other artistic endeavors. They are founding members of Seattle Wholesale Growers Market Cooperative. In fact, Diane has served as board chair since its inception. The Cooperative is one of only a few of its kind in the country, and is limited to farms ½ acre to 20 acres. It's comprised of "growers who are actually doing the farming," Diane explains, and sells wholesale to the trade (restaurants, event planners, photographers, florists, and other businesses) from 6am to noon, five days a week. The Market is also open briefly on Fridays to the public. The Cooperative is a vehicle for bringing locally grown cut flowers and foliage to market, and also provides an opportunity for information sharing and collaboration between the growers.

Over 80 different kinds of flowers and foliage are grown on Jello Mold Farm, including viburnum, ninebark, lilacs, hydrangea, clematis vines, blooming and fruiting branches, raspberry foliage, scabiosa, amaranth, and hellebores. There is an emphasis on unique and decorative foliage, which is in high demand at the Market, but Dennis and Diane grow rows and rows of flowers, too: sweet peas, dahlias, globe thistle, peonies, and poppies, just to name a few.

The farm's name is taken from Diane's art installation of over 500 thrifted jello molds on a run-down building years ago that became an unlikely tourist attraction. The building is long gone, but you can still find jello molds mounted all around the farm.

Dennis and Diane's farming practices focus on both environmental and economic sustainability. The farm is certified salmon safe, which means that it uses only organic-certified fertilizers and pest controls. But it goes well beyond that, utilizing practices such as composting; recycling and careful use of water and other resources; creation and maintenance of healthy soil by rotating crops and preventing erosion; and maintaining wild corridors and growing a diversity of plants to support a wide variety of animal life. Sustainability includes making and paying a living wage, too, so that it is possible to continue

working as farmers, and teaching the skills to others. To support the next generation, Jello Mold Farm offers one-week farm internships, complete with a stipend and room and board, as "an opportunity to immerse yourself in the daily activities of running an intensive and diversified cut flower farm."

In addition to sustainable practices, Jello Mold Farm embraces the importance of buying flowers locally. "We're growing art supplies," and many more options are available when you buy fresh flowers because you're not limited to only those varieties that can travel long distance, Diane explains. This also helps to reduce the carbon footprint. And, buying local flowers is a reminder of time and place – a connection with the season they grew in, and with nature itself.

According to the Jello Mold Farm website, "80% of cut flowers sold in the United States are imported. Most come from countries with cheap labor and less developed environmental standards. Due to global trade agreements, there are no tariffs on imported flowers. Consumers most often do not know where their flowers come from. Our farm is proud to be certified American Grown as part of a joint effort by U.S. flower farmers to raise consumer awareness and help preserve our domestic and local flower farming heritage." ⌘

Jello Mold Farm

Farmers: Dennis Westphall and Diane Szukovathy

Website: jellomoldfarm.com

Instagram: dianeszukovathy

Flowers sold at Seattle Wholesale Growers Market

Inari Okami

By Nele Redweik

Inari Okami is the androgynous Japanese kami or spirit of fertility, rice, tea and agriculture. The duality of the two sides of the hat and the textured rosette stitch, not unlike rice kernels, led me to choose the name.

FINISHED MEASUREMENTS
18.5" circumference
8" tall

MATERIALS
Yarn on the House Big Sister (80% merino/10% cashmere/10% nylon, 231 yds per 100 g)
MC: 1 skein in Mango
CC: 1 skein in Cacao

US 7 (4.5 mm) 16" circular needle and set of double pointed needles (dpns) (shell)
US 6 (4 mm) 16" circular needle and set of dpns (lining)
US 5 (3.75 mm) 16" circular needle (ribbing)
Stitch markers, tapestry needle, waste yarn, crochet hook (optional, for provisional cast on)

GAUGE
20 sts and 28 rows = 4" in rosette stitch with US 7 (4.5 mm) needle, blocked
20 sts and 28 rows = 4" in St st with US 6 (4 mm) needle, blocked

NOTES

Hat is double-layered with a patterned shell and stockinette lining. Shell is knit first, beginning with a provisional cast on. Finished shell is then turned so the reverse of the stitch pattern is the public side. Stitches are picked up from the provisional cast on to knit the lining, which when complete is tucked inside the shell.

ROSETTE STITCH (worked in the round, multiple of 2 sts + 1)

Rnd 1: Purl.
Rnd 2: *P2tog without dropping sts from left needle, then k2tog through same 2 sts and drop from left needle; rep from * to last st, k1.
Rnd 3: Purl.
Rnd 4: K1, *p2tog without dropping sts from left needle, then k2tog through same 2 sts and drop from left needle; rep from * to end.
Rep Rnds 1-4 for pattern.

DIRECTIONS

SHELL

With US 5 (3.75 mm) needle and waste yarn, use a provisional method to CO 92 sts. (Instructions for a crochet provisional CO can be found at the end of this pattern, or use your preferred method.) Change to MC, pm and join to work in the round.
Rib rnd: *K2, p2; rep from * to end.
Rep this rnd until rib measures 2".

Change to US 7 (4.5 mm) circular.
Set-up rnd: M1, *p2tog without dropping sts from left needle, then k2tog through same 2 sts and drop from left needle; rep from * to end. 93 sts.
Work Rnds 1-4 of rosette stitch until hat measures 7'' from CO, ending with Rnd 4.

Shape crown:
Change to dpns when necessary.
Rnd 1 (dec rnd): P2tog, p19, p3tog, *p20, p3tog; rep from * to end. 84 sts remain.
Rnd 2: K1, *p2tog without dropping sts from left needle, then k2tog through same 2 sts and drop from left needle; rep from * to last st, k1.
Rnd 3 (dec rnd): *P4, p3tog; rep from * to end. 60 sts remain.
Rnd 4: *P2tog without dropping sts from left needle, then k2tog through same 2 sts and drop from left needle; rep from *
Rnd 5 (dec rnd): *P3tog; rep from * to end. 20 sts remain.
Rnd 6: Rep Rnd 4.
Rnd 7 (dec rnd): P1, *p3tog; rep from * to last st, p1. 8 sts remain.

Cut yarn, thread through rem sts and cinch closed.

LINING
Turn shell inside out. Remove waste yarn from provisional CO and place resulting 92 sts on US 5 (3.75 mm) circular, preserving the original location of the beginning of the rnd. Join CC, pm, and knit 1 rnd.
Rib rnd: *P2, k2; rep from * to end.
Rep rib rnd until lining ribbing measures 2''.

Change to US 6 (4 mm) circular. Work in St st (knit every rnd) until lining measures 6'' from CO.

Weave in all ends at this point. The next step is to shape the crown and close up the hat, so there won't be another opportunity.

Shape crown:
Change to dpns when necessary.
Set-up rnd: [K11, pm, k10, k2tog, pm] 3 times, k11, pm, k10, k2tog. 88 sts remain.
Knit 1 rnd.
Dec rnd: *Knit to 2 sts before m, k2tog, sl m; rep from * to end. 8 sts dec'd.
Rep dec rnd on every other rnd 2 more times, then on every rnd 7 times. 8 sts remain.

Cut yarn, thread through rem sts and cinch closed. Weave in end by running needle tip through the back of a few stitches. Do not trim close, but leave 1-2" extra to help prevent the end working loose.

FINISHING
Block.
Optional: make a pom pom with the leftover yarn and sew to top of hat.

TECHNIQUES
Crochet Provisional Cast On
With waste yarn, make a slip knot loop on the crochet hook. Holding the knitting needle in your left hand and crochet hook in your right, bring the yarn behind the needle. *With the crochet hook in front of the needle, wrap the yarn over the needle and the hook, and pull loop through. 1 st has been cast on the needle. Bring the yarn back between the needle and hook and repeat from * until you have cast on the required number of stitches. Cut yarn and pull tail through last loop to fasten off. To remove the waste yarn later, pick out the fastened-off end and pull the tail to unravel the chain.

ABBREVIATIONS
CC   contrast color
CO   cast on/cast-on
K   knit
K2tog knit 2 sts together
M   marker
MC   main color
M1   make 1: with right needle, pick up running thread between needles from back to front and place it on left needle, then knit it through the back loop
P   purl
Pm   place marker
P2tog purl 2 sts together
P3tog purl 3 sts together
Rnd   round
St(s)   stitch(es)
St st   stockinette stitch

Twin Falls (above) and Snoqualmie Falls (below) are just two of the waterfalls within easy hiking distance if you're staying at Salish Lodge in Snoqualmie.

A Family Business: YOTH Yarn

Y OTH Yarns is a family affair, explains founder Veronika Jobe. When she decided she wanted to start a yarn company, the first person she went to was her brother, Daniel Burda. Although Daniel was only in his early 20s at the time and still in college, he switched his major to business and saw Veronika's offer as an opportunity to put what he would be learning into practice. Once her brother was on board, Veronika recruited her parents to help. Her mother is an "all-around consultant" and her father builds all of the pieces needed for display and shipping. "My dad is the builder—he's the MacGyver of construction." Veronika's daughter Jasmine has gotten involved by modeling many of the patterns created for YOTH. The importance of family in this business is even reflected in the names of the yarn bases: Father, Mother, Big Sis, Little Bro, Daughter, and the newest yarn line, Best Friend.

One of the most striking characteristics of YOTH yarns is the color palettes. The yarn was hand dyed at first, but the quantities became overwhelming, and now YOTH is dyed at Saco River Dyehouse in Maine, in small batches to so that it retains the look of hand dyed yarn. The colors are subtle and understated, inspired by colors you would find in nature. Instead of just a typical white or brown or gray, for instance, the line features 12 different complex neutrals that showcase the colors of the Pacific Northwest: stormy skies, heavy clouds, silvery rain, loamy earth.

According to Veronika, "we wanted the brand to be very unisex —99% of our colors can be worn by both men and women—and we wanted colors that you would wear or use again and again. We started with the Raw Palette because neutrals are the number one color in most everyone's wardrobe. Next came the blues and greens because these are Pacific Northwest colors and everyone's wardrobe contains a lot of denim shades."

The other unique characteristic of YOTH yarns is that the colors blend with each other beautifully, but are not actually gradients of each other. "We really wanted colors that worked well together – you can close your eyes and pick up two skeins of yarn and they'll look good," notes Veronika. "When we were developing color palettes, we wanted them to be shades of each other, but not straight gradients. Each color is beautiful in and of itself."

The yarn color names themselves make you want to knit with YOTH. "They're inspired by foods, because we love knitting and eating," laughs Veronika. The YOTH website states that they "are as delicious to the eye as they are to knit." The Raw Palette includes names such as oyster, caviar, cacao, and hazelnut; the Fresh Palette includes concord grape, kale, and thyme; and the Juicy Palette includes carrot, celery, raw honey, and mango. Next, YOTH will be releasing the Roots Palette, in shades of reds, pinks, and purples.

Recently YOTH has branched out to create several "sheepy" yarn lines in natural colors, as well. Veronika

YOTH Yarn

Yarnists: Veronika Jobe and Daniel Burda

Website: yothyarn.com

Instagram: yarnonthehouse

Yarn Lines: Father (worsted), Mother (lace), Big Sis (DK), Little Bro (Fingering), Daughter (worsted) and Best Friend (light fingering)

describes Best Friend and Daughter as "rustic, weathered and earthy, true and just really wooly." These lines have been developed in collaboration with Cestari Sheep & Wool Company, a family-run sheep operation in Virginia that has been in business since 1946.

These days YOTH (which stands for Yarn On The House, the name of Veronika's original yarn blog) continues to grow. Daniel handles all of the stock, receiving, finances and financial planning, and does a lot of the travel. Veronika is in charge of branding, marketing, social media, designing and collaborating with other designers, and making connections and networking. In addition to the upcoming release of the Roots Palette, YOTH is regularly releasing new patterns and dedicates a lot of time on the road, to trunk shows and events such as Stitches West.

Veronika credits her close-knit family and the relationship she built with women she met while working at Tolt Yarn and Wool with giving her the courage to leave a corporate job and pursue something she felt passionate about. "For me," she says, "it's about collaboration and community. It's hanging out with our friends and doing things we love." ⌘

Fern and Feather

Top down Icelanic-inspired stranded yoke sweater
By Jennifer Steingass

SIZES
A (B, C, D, E) (F, G, H, I) (J, K, L)

FINISHED MEASUREMENTS
Bust 30.75 (33, 35.5, 39, 41) (43.5, 46.25, 49, 51.5) (54.25, 57.25, 59.5)"/78 (84, 90, 99, 104) (110.5, 117.5, 124.5, 131) (138, 145.5, 151) cm

Length from back neck 23.25   (23.5, 23.75, 24, 24, 24.25, 24.25, 24.5, 24.5, 24.75, 25, 25.25)"/59 (59.5, 60.5, 61, 61) (61.5, 61.5, 62, 62, 63, 63.5, 64) cm

Shown with 4" positive ease.

MATERIALS
Yarn on the House Yarns Father (100% American Rambouillet wool, 220 yds/201 m per 100 g)
MC: 4 (4, 5, 5, 5) (5, 6, 6, 7) (7, 8, 8) skeins in Wheatgrass
CC: 1 skein (all sizes) in Sea Salt

Substitute with another worsted weight wool yarn.
MC: 750 (800, 875, 950, 1000) (1070, 1250, 1310, 1400) (1500, 1570, 1600) yds/686 (732, 801, 869, 915, 979, 1143, 1198, 1281, 1372, 1436, 1464) m
CC: 85 (90, 100, 110, 120) (130, 140, 150, 160) (170, 180, 190) yds/78 (83, 92, 101, 110) (119, 128, 138, 147) (156, 165, 174) m

A needle: US 4 (3.5 mm) double pointed needles or 16"/40 cm circular (neckline)
B needle: US 5 (3.75 mm) double pointed needles and 24"/60 cm or longer circular (ribbed edges)
C needle: US 6 (4 mm) double pointed needles, 16"/40 cm circular, and 24"/60 cm or longer circular (main body)
Stitch markers in four colors, tapestry needle, waste yarn, removable marker

GAUGE
18 sts and 28 rnds = 4" in stockinette st in the round on C needles, blocked
18 sts and 25 rnds = 4" in charted pattern on C needles, blocked

NOTES
Pullover is worked seamlessly from the top down, starting with a simple rolled neckline. The yoke is knit in stranded color work, then short row shaping is added to the back of the sweater to shape the shoulders and neckline. Gentle waist shaping makes for a flattering, feminine fit.

Read chart from right to left. For optimal color dominance, hold the CC strand to the left and the MC strand to the right.

SPECIAL STITCHES

Inv-L – invisible increase left: sl next st pwise with yarn in back, then place the left leg of the st in the row below the slipped st on the left needle and knit it through the back loop

Inv-R – invisible right increase: place the right leg of the st in the row below next st onto left needle and knit it, then sl next st pwise with yarn in back

DIRECTIONS
YOKE

With MC and size A needle(s), use the long-tail method to CO 62 (66, 72, 78, 80) (84, 90, 92, 98) (104, 108, 110) sts. Pm color A and join to work in the round. Rnds begin behind the left shoulder.

Knit 1 rnd.

Sizes A (–, –, –, E) (–, –, H, I) (J, –, L) only:
Next rnd: K9 (–, –, –, 12) (–, –, 14, 15) (16, –, 17), Inv-L (see Special Stitches)] 6 times, knit to last st, Inv-L. 7 sts inc'd.

Sizes – (B, C, D, –) (F, G, –, –) (–, K, –)'' only:
Next rnd: [K – (10, 11, 12, –) (13, 14, –, –) (–, 17, –), Inv-L (see Special Stitches)] 6 times. 6 sts inc'd.

All sizes:
69 (72, 78, 84, 87) (90, 96, 99, 105) (111, 114, 117) sts on the needle.
　　　　　　Knit 2 rnds.

Change to shorter C circular needle. Join CC. Work Rnds 1–39 of yoke chart (see Notes), changing to longer circular needle when necessary. 207 (216, 234, 252, 261) (270, 288, 297, 315) (333, 342, 351) sts. Break CC and continue with MC only.

Knit 1 rnd.

Sizes A (–, –, –, E) (–, –, H, I) (J, –, L) only:
Next rnd: K1, k2tog, knit to end.

Sizes – (B, C, D, –) (F, G, –, –) (–, K, –)'' only:
Knit 1 rnd.

All sizes:
206 (216, 234, 252, 260) (270, 288, 296, 314) (332, 342, 350) sts on needle.

Place markers for short row shaping and body and sleeve separation as follows: K63 (66, 71, 78, 81) (85, 91, 94, 100) (105, 110, 113) [back], pm color B, k40 (42, 46, 48, 49) (50, 53, 54, 57) (61, 61, 62) [right sleeve], pm color C, k63 (66, 71, 78, 81) (85, 91, 94, 100) (105, 110, 113) [front], pm color D, k40 (42, 46, 48, 49) (50, 53, 54, 57) (61, 61, 62) [left sleeve] to end of rnd.

Work even, if necessary, until yoke measures 6.75 (7, 7.25, 7.5, 7.5) (7.75, 7.75, 8, 8) (8.25, 8.5, 8.75)''/17 (18, 18.5, 19, 19) (19.5, 19.5, 20.5, 20.5) (21, 21.5, 22) cm from rolled neck edge.

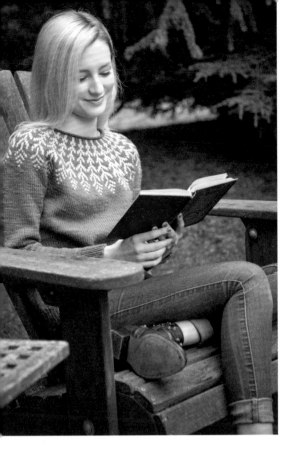

Short row shaping:
Note: Short rows have been written with the wrap and turn (w&t) method in mind, but you may substitute any other method that you prefer.

Short row 1 (RS): Knit across back to marker B, sl m, knit across right sleeve to marker C, sl m, k6, w&t.
Short row 2 (WS): Purl to marker C, sl m, purl across right sleeve to marker B, sl m, purl across back to marker A, sl m, purl across left sleeve to marker D, sl m, p6, w&t.
Short row 3: Knit to marker D, sl m, knit across left sleeve to marker A, sl m, knit across back to marker B, sl m, knit across right sleeve to 2 sts before marker C, w&t.
Short row 4: Purl across right sleeve to marker B, sl m, purl across back to marker A, sl m, purl across left sleeve to 2 sts before marker D, w&t.
Short row 5: Knit across left sleeve to marker A, sl m, knit across back to marker B, sl m, knit to 8 sts before marker C, w&t.
Short row 6: Purl across right sleeve to marker B, sl m, purl across back to marker A, sl m, purl to 8 sts before marker D, w&t.
Next row: Knit to marker A/end of rnd, picking up and knitting wraps tog with wrapped sts.
Next rnd: Knit 1 complete rnd, picking up and knitting rem wraps tog with wrapped sts.

Separate body and sleeves:
Remove marker A (beg of rnd). Knit across back to marker B and remove it. Place next 40 (42, 46, 48, 49) (50, 53, 54, 57) (61, 61, 62) sts on waste yarn for right sleeve. Remove marker C. Use the backward loop method to CO 3 (4, 5, 5, 6) (7, 7, 8, 8) (9, 10, 11) sts for underarm, pm color B for side, CO 3 (4, 4, 5, 5) (6, 6, 8, 8) (8, 9, 10) more underarm sts. Knit across front to marker D and remove it. Place next 40 (42, 46, 48, 49) (50, 53, 54, 57) (61, 61, 62) sts on waste yarn for left sleeve. Use the backward loop method to CO 3 (4, 5, 5, 6) (7, 7, 8, 8) (9, 10, 11) sts for underarm, pm color A for side and new beg of rnd, CO 3 (4, 4, 5, 5) (6, 6, 8, 8) (8, 9, 10) more underarm sts. 138 (148, 160, 176, 184) (196, 208, 220, 232) (244, 258, 268) sts on needle: 69 (74, 80, 88, 92) (98, 104, 110, 116) (122, 129, 134) each for front and back. Rnds begin at the left underarm. Place a removable marker in the row just completed, at center front of body, and leave it there as a point to measure from.

LOWER BODY
Knit 1 rnd.

Short row shaping:
Short row 1 (RS): Knit across back to marker B, sl m, k6, w&t.
Short row 2 (WS): Purl to marker B, sl m, purl across back to marker A, sl m, p6, w&t.
Short row 3: Knit to marker A, sl m, knit across back to 2 sts before marker B, w&t.
Short row 4: Purl to 2 sts before marker A, w&t.
Short row 5: Knit to 8 sts before marker B, w&t.
Short row 6: Purl to 8 sts before marker A, w&t.
Next rnd: Knit to end of rnd/marker A, picking up and knitting wraps together with wrapped sts.
Next rnd: Knit to end of rnd, picking up and knitting remaining wraps together with wrapped sts.

Work even until front of body measures 1.5''/4 cm from marked row.

Shape waist:
Dec rnd: [K6, k2tog, knit to 8 sts before m, ssk, k6, sl m] 2 times. 4 sts dec'd.
Rep dec rnd on every 9th rnd 3 more times. 122 (132, 144, 160, 168) (180, 192, 204, 216) (228, 242, 252) sts rem.

Work even until front of body measures 6.5''/16.5 cm from marked row.

Inc rnd: [K6, Inv-R, knit to 7 sts before m, Inv-L, k6, sl m] 2 times. 4 sts inc'd.

Rep inc rnd on every 7th rnd 5 more times. 146 (156, 168, 184, 192) (204, 216, 228, 240) (252, 266, 276) sts.

Work even until front of body measures 12.5"/32 cm from marked row, or 2"/5 cm less than desired total length.

Change to B circular needle.
Rib rnd: *K1, p1; rep from * to end.
Rep this rnd until rib measures 2".
BO all sts in rib.

SLEEVES
Transfer 40 (42, 46, 48, 49) (50, 53, 54, 57) (61, 61, 62) sleeve sts from waste yarn to a spare needle.

With RS facing, join MC at right end of underarm CO sts on body. With size C dpns or shorter circular needle, pick up and knit 3 (4, 5, 5, 6) (7, 7, 8, 8) (9, 10, 11) sts from CO edge, pm for beg of rnd, pick up and knit 3 (4, 4, 5, 5) (6, 6, 8, 8) (8, 9, 10) more sts from CO edge, then pick up and knit 2 sts in the corner between the CO and the sleeve. Knit across the sleeve sts from spare needle, then pick up and knit 2 sts in the corner, knit to end of rnd. 50 (54, 59, 62, 64) (67, 70, 74, 77) (82, 84, 87) total sleeve sts.

Work even in stockinette until sleeve measures 2 (2, 2, 2, 2) (2, 1.5, 1.5, 1.5) (1.5, 1.5, 1)"/ 5 (5, 5, 5, 5) (5, 4, 4, 4) (4, 4, 2.5) cm from underarm.

Dec rnd: K4, k2tog, knit to last 6 sts, ssk, k4. 2 sts dec'd.
Rep dec rnd on every 15 (13, 10, 9, 8) (8, 8, 7, 7) (6, 6, 6)th rnd 6 (7, 9, 10, 11) (11, 12, 13, 14) (16, 16, 17) more times, changing to dpns when/if necessary. 36 (38, 39, 40, 40) (43, 44, 46, 47) (48, 50, 51) sts rem.

Work even until sleeve measures 16"/40.5 cm from underarm, or 2"/5 cm less than desired total length, decreasing 0 (0, 1, 0, 0) (1, 0, 0, 1) (0, 0, 1) st inconspicuously on last rnd. 36 (38, 38, 40, 40) (42, 44, 46, 46) (48, 50, 50) sts rem.

Change to B dpns.
Rib rnd: *K1, p1; rep from * to end.
Rep this rnd until rib measures 2"/5 cm. BO all sts in rib.

FINISHING
Weave in ends. Block.

TECHNIQUES

Wrap and Turn for Short Rows (w&t)

On a RS row: Slip the next st pwise wyib, bring yarn to front between needles, return slipped st to left needle, turn work.

On a WS row: Slip the next st pwise wyif, bring yarn to back between needles, return slipped st to left needle, turn work.

ABBREVIATIONS

BO – bind off, bound–off

CC – contrast color

CO – cast on, cast–on

Dec('d) – decrease(d)

Inc('d) – increase(d)

K – knit

K2tog – knit 2 sts together

M – marker

MC – main color

P – purl

Pm – place marker

Pwise – purlwise/as if to purl

Rem – remain

Rep – repeat

Rnd(s) – round(s)

RS – right side

Sl – slip

Ssk – [sl 1 as if to knit] 2 times, insert left needle into these 2 sts and knit them together

St(s) – stitch(es)

St st – stockinette stitch

W&t – wrap and turn (see Techniques)

WS – wrong side

Fern and Feather

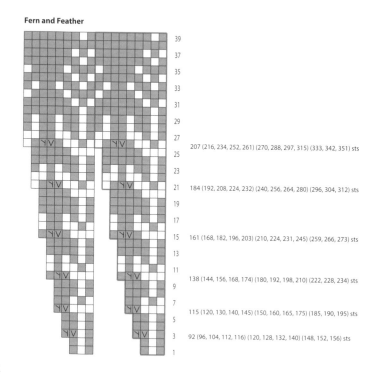

207 (216, 234, 252, 261) (270, 288, 297, 315) (333, 342, 351) sts

184 (192, 208, 224, 232) (240, 256, 264, 280) (296, 304, 312) sts

161 (168, 182, 196, 203) (210, 224, 231, 245) (259, 266, 273) sts

138 (144, 156, 168, 174) (180, 192, 198, 210) (222, 228, 234) sts

115 (120, 130, 140, 145) (150, 160, 165, 175) (185, 190, 195) sts

92 (96, 104, 112, 116) (120, 128, 132, 140) (148, 152, 156) sts

Key

knit with MC

knit with CC

Inv-L increase (see Special Stitches) with MC

pattern repeat

SCHEMATIC MEASUREMENTS

A neck circumference	13.75	14.75	16	17.25	17.75	18.75	20	20.5	21.75	23	24	24.5	in
	35	37.5	40.5	44	45	47.5	51	52	55	58.5	61	62	cm
B yoke depth front	6.75	7	7.25	7.5	7.5	7.75	7.75	8	8	8.25	8.5	8.75	in
	17	18	18.5	19	19	19.5	19.5	20.5	20.5	21	21.5	22	cm
C bust circumference	30.75	33	35.5	39	41	43.5	46.25	49	51.5	54.25	57.25	59.5	in
	78	84	90	99	104	110.5	117.5	124.5	131	138	145.5	151	cm
D waist circumference	27	29.25	32	35.5	37.25	40	42.75	45.25	48	50.75	53.75	56	in
	68.5	74.5	81.5	90	94.5	101.5	108.5	115	122	129	136.5	142	cm
E hip circumference	32.5	34.75	37.25	41	42.75	45.25	48	50.75	53.25	56	59	61.25	in
	82.5	88.5	94.5	104	108.5	115	122	129	135.5	142	150	155.5	cm
F upper sleeve circumference	11	12	13	13.75	14.25	15	15.5	16.5	17	18.25	18.75	19.25	in
	28	30.5	33	35	36	38	39.5	42	43	46.5	47.5	49	cm
G cuff circumference	8	8.5	8.5	9	9	9.25	9.75	10.25	10.25	10.75	11	11	in
	20.5	21.5	21.5	23	23	23.5	25	26	26	27.5	28	28	cm
H back length from neck (over short rows)	23.25	23.5	23.75	24	24	24.25	24.25	24.5	24.5	24.75	25	25.25	in
	59	59.5	60.5	61	61	61.5	61.5	62	62	63	63.5	64	cm

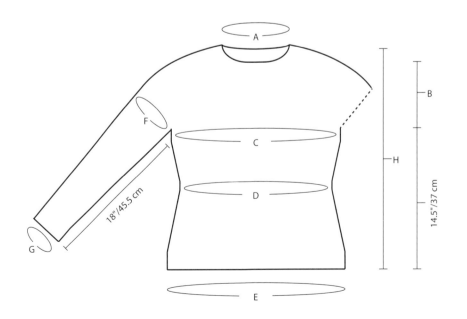

Dyed in the Wool: Spincycle Yarns

Spincycle dyeing duo Kate Burge and Rachel Price tell me that they achieve Spincycle's color aesthetic through a "punk rock dyeing process." "We don't weigh out our dye powder. We have recipes and colors that repeat, but it's still really just from the gut," Rachel says. "We do dye everything in the wool—which means the wool is dyed before it's spun—that's how you get that long, unpredictable dyeing shift. It's a hand spinners' dyeing process."

Kate goes on to explain that most milled yarn is either dyed before it's ever carded or processed, or it's dyed after it's skeined. "Ours is one of the only painted rovings. It's definitely the hardest way but it's worth it, because each skein is a mini work of art." For instance, Kate explains that to achieve one of their newest lines of colors, called Truth Bomb, she paints black and silver "like clouds" toward the top of the roving, and "then I paint a rainbow down the rest of it." The result is a totally unique, one-of-kind skein of rainbow colors.

Rachel and Kate were both already dyeing and spinning when they met at a food co-op in Bellingham over a decade ago. The two were making more yarn than they needed for their own knitting, so they teamed up to sell skeins at the farmer's market. The company is named for the bike trailers that the two used to haul yarn to the farmers market each week. At that time, their style of yarn—with a more rustic, natural hand—wasn't readily available. Soon the two were in business together, making all of their yarn by hand for the first six years. "We were really fast and really good at making handspun yarn, and able to make a living at it, but then we had our babies and we didn't have the time or energy to handspin or travel for yarn shows and events," explains Rachel. This change in lifestyle, along with a chance meeting with a woman opening up a fiber mill on Camano Island, led to Spincycle's small batch mill production. That first yarn, which became the Dyed in the Wool line, was followed

by others, including a worsted weight yarn and a hand plied super bulky.

Spincycle's slow growth model—building up a clientele over years of production, careful managing of finances and avoidance of debt—placed the company in a position to turn a sudden change of events into an opportunity when the Camano Island mill owner decided in early summer of this year to sell. "It was a 'do or die' moment," describes Rachel. "So we decided to buy the mill." In order to house the mill in Bellingham, the team acquired warehouse space, so now the mill, storage, dye studio, and drying room will all be under one roof.

In addition to the convenience of one central location, this development will give Spincycle more flexibility to develop different yarn bases. "We'd love to work with local farmers and do short runs of heirloom, single breed yarns," says Kate. "It's been hard to develop different yarn lines because the mill has been far enough away that it can be a long, drawn-out complicated process of trial and error. Now, we can make changes in real time and play around with it a lot more."

The Spincycle yarn tags—written by Rachel and adorned with the company's pirate sheep logo—help to explain the color aesthetic: "... colors meet and part ways in stunning, unique combinations; the overall effect is of a balanced, seamless whole. Color changes are always brilliant, never repetitive." Color names, such as Mississippi Marsala, Pick Your Poison, Shades of Earth, and Salty Dog, are as unique as the yarns themselves. The result is a wholly creative yarn that challenges knitters and fiber enthusiasts to think about color in new and different ways. ⌘

Spincycle

Spinsters: Kate Burge and Rachel Price

Website: spincycleyarns.com

Instagram: spincycle_yarns

Yarn Lines: Dyed In The Wool, Versus, Independence, Knit Fast Die Young

Alki Beach Hoodie

By Andrea Hungerford

In order to style this like a traditional baja beach hoodie, I incorporated vertical stripes by knitting the hoodie side-to-side in one piece. The color shifting in the stripes is created by double-stranding Spincycle yarn, so that the yarn knits up in marled color changes. I love this effect and it beautifully showcases how creatively you can use Spincycle yarns! The body of the hoodie is knit in Cestari's Ash Lawn yarn – an ideal combination of wool and cotton, it is sturdy yet also so next-to-skin soft that even the most sensitive little ones will be sure to love wearing it.

SIZES
Age 4 (6, 8, 10) years
Approx. chest measurement 23 (25, 26.5, 28)"
Shown in sizes 4 and 8

FINISHED MEASUREMENTS
Chest circumference 28 (30.5, 31.5, 33.5)"
Length from shoulder (hemmed) 14 (15.5, 18.25, 19.5)"

MATERIALS
MC: Cestari Ash Lawn Collection 3 Ply DK weight (75% cotton/25% wool, 250 yds per 100 g), 3 (3, 3, 4) skeins in Natural White
CC: Spincycle Dyed in the Wool (100% superwash American wool, 200 yds per 54 g), 2 (2, 2, 3) skeins in Robin's Egg (blue) or Heart Sigh (pink)

US 6 (4 mm) 24" circular needle, stitch holders, tapestry needle, stitch marker

GAUGE
19 sts and 28 rows = 4" in stripe pattern with 1 strand of MC and 2 strands of CC, blocked

NOTES
Knit cuff-to-cuff in one piece.
Always use MC single-stranded and CC double-stranded.
Finished chest circumference reflects measurement after seaming. Measurements on schematic are before seaming and hemming.

STRIPE PATTERN
Stripe pattern repeats over 30 rows. Odd-numbered rows are WS, even-numbered rows are RS.

Rows 1-16: With MC and beg with a purl row (WS), work 16 rows stockinette.
Row 17 (WS): With CC held double, knit.
Rows 18-21: With MC and beg with a knit row (RS), work 4 rows stockinette.
Rows 22-25: With CC held double and beg with a knit row (RS), work 4 rows stockinette.
Rows 26-29: With MC and beg with a knit row (RS), work 4 rows stockinette.
Row 30 (RS): With CC held double, purl.

MC should be joined before Rows 1 and 18 and cut after Rows 16 and 29; otherwise, carry it up the side of the work when not in use. CC should be joined before Row 17 and cut after Row 30; otherwise, carry it up the side of the work when not in use.

DIRECTIONS
LEFT SLEEVE
Cuff: With MC, CO 33 (35, 37, 39) sts. Knit 9 rows, ending with a WS row.

Begin stripes and shape sleeve:
Work in stripe patt beg with Row 28 (8, 26, 12) (RS). AT THE SAME TIME, beginning on the 7th row above the cuff, work increases:
Inc row (RS): Work 2 sts, m1 (if a knit row) or m1P (if a purl row), work to last 2 sts, m1 or m1P, work to end. 2 sts inc'd.
Rep inc row on every 6th row 2 (2, 5, 8) more times, then on every 8th row 5 (7, 6, 5) times. 49 (55, 61, 67) sts.
Work 7 rows even, ending with a WS row (Row 3 [29, 27, 23] of stripe patt.)

LEFT SIDE BODY
Use the cable method to CO 49 (53, 63, 67) sts at beg of next 2 rows. 147 (161, 187, 201) sts.
Work 30 (32, 34, 36) rows even, ending with a WS row (Row 5 [3, 3, 1] of stripe patt.)

CENTER BODY
Divide front and back (RS): K73 (80, 93, 100) and place these sts on a holder for back, BO 4 (2, 4, 2) sts, work to end. 70 (79, 90, 99) sts rem for front.

Shape front neck:
Working on front sts only, BO 2 sts at beg of next 8 (9, 9, 10) RS rows. 54 (61, 72, 79) sts rem. (Last row worked should be Row 22 of stripe patt.)
Work 2 rows even, ending with a RS row.
Use the backward loop method to CO 2 sts at end of next 8 (9, 9, 10) WS rows. 70 (79, 90, 99) sts.
Work 1 RS row even (Row 10 [12, 12, 14] of stripe patt).
Place sts on a holder but do not cut yarn.

Back neck:
Replace 73 (80, 93, 100) held back sts on needle and join yarn with WS facing. Work 34 (38, 38, 42) rows even, ending with a WS row (Row 10 [12, 12, 14] of stripe pattern). Cut yarn and place sts on a holder.

Rejoin front and back (WS): Return front sts to needle with WS facing. Work across front sts, use the backward loop method to CO 5 (3, 5, 3) sts on right needle, pm, transfer held back sts to left needle tip with WS facing and work to end. 148 (162, 188, 202) sts.

RIGHT SIDE BODY
Next row (RS): Work to 1 st before m, k2tog (removing m), work to end. 147 (161, 187, 201) sts.
Work 29 (31, 33, 35) rows even, ending with a WS row (Row 11 [15, 17, 21] of stripe patt.)
BO 49 (53, 63, 67) sts at beg of next 2 rows. 49 (55, 61, 67) sts rem.

RIGHT SLEEVE
Shape sleeve:
Work 8 rows even, ending with a WS row (Row 21 (25, 27, 1) of stripe patt.)
Dec row (RS): Work 2 sts, ssk (if a knit row) or p2tog (if a purl row), work to last 4 sts, k2tog (knit row) or p2tog (purl row), work to end. 2 sts dec'd.
Rep dec row on every 8th row 5 (7, 6, 5) more times, then on every 6th row 2 (2, 5, 8) times. 33 (35, 37, 39) sts rem.
Work 5 rows even, ending with a WS row (Row 19 [9, 21, 5] of stripe patt).

Cuff:
With MC, purl 9 rows.
BO in purl on WS.
Block piece to schematic measurements.

HOOD

With MC, CO 5 sts, then beg at base of V-neck with RS facing pick up and knit 36 (38, 40, 42) sts around right neckline to center back, pm, pick up and knit 36 (38, 40, 42) sts around left neckline to base of V-neck, then use the backward loop method to CO 5 more sts on right needle. 82 (86, 90, 94) sts.

Beg working in stripe patt with Row 1 (WS). AT THE SAME TIME, beginning on first RS row, shape hood:
Inc row (RS): Work to 2 sts before m, m1, k2, sl m, k2, m1, work to end. 2 sts inc'd.
Rep inc row on every RS row 3 more times. 90 (94, 98, 102) sts.
Work even until hood measures 8.5 (9.5, 9.5, 10.5)" from pick-up row, ending with a WS row.
Dec row (RS): Work to 2 sts before m, k2tog (on a knit row) or p2tog (on a purl row), sl m, ssk (knit row) or p2tog (purl row), work to end. 2 sts dec'd.
Rep dec row on every RS row until hood measures 11 (12, 12, 13)" from pick-up row.
Place each half of the hood stitches on a separate needle. With wrong sides facing each other, join the two halves using a 3-needle BO.

FINISHING

Block hood. Fold the extra 5 sts at each end of hood to the inside and slip stitch the long edge in place to make the drawstring casing, leaving the short ends open. Using 2 strands of CC, CO 2 sts. *K2, do not turn. Slip sts from right needle tip to left and draw yarn snugly across back of work. Repeat from * until cord measures 30 (34, 34, 38)". BO and weave in ends. Use a safety pin to run the drawstring through the casing, then knot each end to prevent the string from being pulled out.

Sew side and sleeve seams. Fold bottom 1.5" of body to WS and slip stitch in place for hem. (You can adjust the length here if desired by taking a shallower or deeper hem, or even leave it unhemmed in case of a sudden growth spurt!) Steam-block seams, hem, and drawstring casing.

TECHNIQUES

3-Needle Bind Off

Have the two pieces to be joined on separate needles held together in the left hand. Using a third needle, insert into first st on front needle, then first st on back needle and knit them together. *Insert into next st on front needle, then next st on back needle and knit them together, then pass first st on right needle over second to BO 1 st. Repeat from *.

ABBREVIATIONS

BO	bind off	CC	contrast color
CO	cast on	dec(s/'d)	decrease(s)/decreased
inc(s/'d)	increase(s)/increased	k	knit
k2tog	knit 2 together	m	marker

m1   make 1: with right needle, pick up running thread between needles from back to front and place it on left needle, then knit it through the back loop

m1P   make 1 purl: with right needle, pick up running thread between needles from front to back, place on left needle, purl it through the front loop.

MC	main color	p	purl
p2tog	purl 2 together	patt	pattern
pm	place marker	rem	remain(s)
rep	repeat	RS	right side

ssk   [slip 1 as if to knit] 2 times, insert left needle into fronts of these sts and knit them together

St st	stockinette stitch	st(s)	stitch(es)
WS	wrong side		

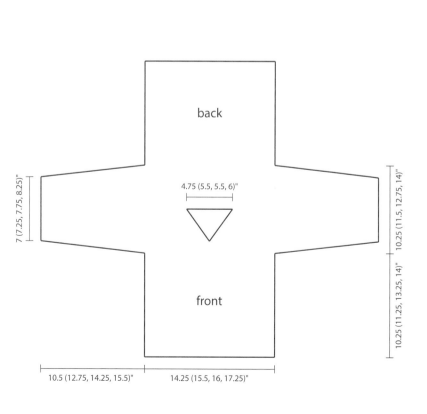

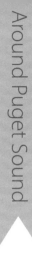

Delicious farm-to-table (and sea-to-table) dishes at Etta's Seafood (above), and a view of the Space Needle from a vantagepoint along the Seattle Art Museum's Olympic Sculpture Park (below).

Local Fiber Mill: Abundant Earth Fiber

Abundant Earth Fiber is located on bucolic Whidbey Island, a 30-minute ferry ride from the Seattle metro area mainland. It's housed in an unassuming building that from the front doesn't hint at the rooms of machinery and tons of bales of wool contained within. Walking through those rooms is an education in how wool becomes yarn: the washing and drying room, the hulking picker, carder, and pin drafter machinery, and the giant spin frames that take up an entire room of their own. "If you want a picture of what I actually do, I need to be holding a wrench," laughs owner Lydia Christiansen.

After three years of operation, Lydia lists "things I've figured out" for me:

Quality matters: "In a small scale yarn business, if we're going to make it, we're not going to compete on volume and price. We have to compete on quality, by creating a superior product. The only way to have a quality product is to take time, make mistakes, and learn from them. It takes time and you have to be committed to it in the long term."

Efficiency: "If you're making mistakes all day long, that costs money. There's no room for sloppiness."

Some form of innovation: "It has to be a routine expectation that you're going to change everything."

Lydia's foray into the world of yarn milling began when she was working as a school teacher on Whidbey Island and her husband gave her a spinning wheel. After teaching herself how to spin, "the wheel led me to the loom, and then I wanted to learn how to turn my neighbors' sheep into wool." Again without

any formal training, she began with washing the wool and slowly taught herself the process of turning wool into yarn. "It got to the point where we had hundreds of pounds of wool in the garage, yarn was hanging in every room in the house . . . finally I said, I think I might need a mill, and then everything just happened so fast." Connections led to opportunities, and Lydia found herself in Oklahoma buying equipment, and then spent four memorable days at Stonehenge Fiber Mill in Michigan. "I found my mentor in Chuck McDermott, and all the people there were so generous with their knowledge and time."

The first two years brought a great deal of trial and error, and some hard lessons about the financial feasibility of a small mill. "Six months into my business, I concluded that the farmers weren't making enough for their wool, and I was working too hard and not making enough. I had to make changes." So she continued to tweak operations and try new approaches. Throughout the challenges, Lydia says that she remains passionate about and inspired by the work. As her website articulates, "we live in a world predominantly unaware of the true cost to humanity for inexpensive textiles. I am broken-hearted, inspired, and committed to projects that move us towards healing for the greater good . . . At the heart of my work is the belief that the earth gives abundantly for us to thrive."

Hope exists in the burgeoning movement that Lydia sees toward breed-specific local and domestic yarns. Much of her milling goes toward production of her own line of yarns, all of which showcase natural undyed colors (only her rovings, made from the sheep at the farm up the road, are dyed). She has several permanent yarn lines,

Abundant Earth Fiber

Mill owner: Lydia Christiansen

Website: abundantearthfiber.com

Instagram: abundantearthfiber

Address: 6438 Central Ave., Clinton

including Josef & Anni, each batch of which is milled from just one or two sheep, creating either a cool gray tone (pepper) or a warm brown (cinnamon). She also produces three gauges of American merino: Native Voice, Sacred Ground, and United Tribe. These yarns will soon be created by blending American merino with 20% Pacific Northwest sourced wool.

In addition, every three months Abundant Earth Fiber turns out a limited edition batch of two or three different yarns. These small-batch yarns showcase different combinations of merino, alpaca, mohair, and other animal fibers. The Abundant Earth Fiber yarns are sold online and at regional yarn shows and events. Lydia also does some limited milling for local yarn producers, including Local Color Fiber Studio, Tolt Yarn and Wool, and Spincycle.

Always eager to take on a new challenge, Lydia says that "I think education is my next push. We have a hand spinning class coming up, where people can come to learn to make fiber together. I always get calls from local farms that say, I have a few alpacas, what do I do with the fleece? I think the answer is, come spend a Saturday with me and I'll teach you how to wash it and recognize if it's worth making into yarn, then next year you can bring me clean and curated fleeces, and I'll card and spin it for you. I would call it Wool Prep 101 for local farms." Abundant Earth currently offers a "Wool Laundry Workshop," which according to the website is a chance to "scour up to two of your own fleeces in our washroom and learn what to expect from your fiber in the process." Also offered is a workshop titled "Have You Any Wool?", where participants will "learn how to see quality in raw fiber . . . we'll even skirt and grade up to four of your own fleeces in the process."

Holding the Abundant Earth Fiber skeins in your hands and reading on the labels about the sheep they're produced from is the best way to get a sense of why this yarn is so special, and why local and sustainable production fundamentally changes the substance of our knitting material. Lydia articulates this feeling: "If you love your craft, you will love your materials. If you love your materials, you will care for the source. I'm seeing knitters want to know more about the source of their yarn and wanting to elevate the quality of their supplies. They want to know what's the best and why it's the best." ⌘

Whidbey Island

Whidbey Island is just a ferry ride from Mukiteo (north of Seattle) or Port Townsend (on the Olympic Peninsula). Or cross the awe-inspiring bridge at Deception Pass on the north end of the island. Once on Whidbey, breathtaking sunrise and sunset water views are everywhere, as is a wide variety of wildlife. The little town of Langley is a charming place to grab a cup of coffee at the Useless Bay Coffee Co., and blow your own glass souvenir at Firehouse Glass Gallery. Be sure to visit Lavender Wind Farm (top left), and don't miss the cinnamon rolls and view of Penn Cove at Knead and Feed in Coupeville!

Pike Stout Poncho

By Thea Colman

SIZES
S (M, L)

FINISHED MEASUREMENTS
45 (49, 55)'' circumference measured 10 (11, 12)'' below high point of shoulder (approx. bust level)
26.75 (30, 32.5)'' long from high point of shoulder to lowest point of back/front
Intended to be worn with plenty of ease.

MATERIALS
Insouciant Fibers heavy worsted weight (100% Romney wool, 175 yds per 100 g), 6 (7, 8) skeins [available at Churchmouse Yarns & Teas, Tolt Yarn and Wool, and insouciantfibers.com]
If substituting yarn, look for a natural fiber, heavy worsted/Aran weight. A lofty or woolen-spun yarn without a lot of weight or drape will come closest to the original.

US 7 (4.5 mm) 16'' circular
US 8 (5 mm) 16'' and 32'' circulars
Cable needle (cn), stitch markers, tapestry needle, stitch holders

GAUGE
16 sts and 24 rows = 4'' in St st and k2, p3 rib on larger needles, blocked.
20 sts and 28 rows = 4'' in k2, p2 rib on smaller needles, blocked.
56-st cable panel measures 9'' wide on larger needles, blocked.

NOTES
Poncho is worked from the top down in one piece to the waist. Poncho body is separated below waist, then short rows are used to give the front and back deep curved hems. Sleeves below waist are worked flat with slight shaping. Edges of lower sleeves are seamed to bottom edges of front and back, then the cuff is seamed closed separately.

To modify width, add extra shaping on center cable side of purl panels, spaced evenly as you work down body. To modify length, add more rows before separating body and sleeves, but

don't go too far past waist/elbow level or the poncho will bunch up when worn.

DIRECTIONS
COLLAR

With smaller needle, CO 124 (132, 136) sts, pm and join to work in the rnd.

Rib rnd: *K2, p2; rep from * to end.

Rep rib rnd until collar measures 8". Change to larger 16" needle.

Next rnd: Work 18 (20, 20) sts in rib [right sleeve], pm, work 44 (46,

48) sts in rib [front], pm, [work 18 (20, 20) sts in rib [left sleeve], pm, work 44 (46, 48) sts to end [back].

BODY

Begin body and shape neck with short rows:

In this section you will increase at the marked "seamlines" while working short rows across the back and sleeve sections to shape the neck. The Cable Set-Up A chart will be worked over the back only.

Short row 1 (RS): K2, m1L, knit across right sleeve to 2 sts before m, m1R, k2, sl m, pfb, w&t. 2 sts inc'd on right sleeve and 1 st inc'd on right front.

Short row 2 (WS): P1, k1, sl m, purl across right sleeve, sl m, kfb, work Row 1 of Cable Set-Up A chart as indicated for your size over 42 (44, 46) sts, kfb, sl m, p2, m1P, purl across left sleeve to 2 sts before m, m1P, k2, sl m, kfb, w&t. 2 sts inc'd on back, 2 sts inc'd on left sleeve, and 1 st inc'd on left front.

Short row 3 (RS): K1, p1, sl m, knit across left sleeve, sl m, p1, work Row 2 of chart as indicated for your size over 44 (46, 48) sts, p1, sl m, k2, m1L, knit across right sleeve to 2 sts before m, m1R, k2, sl m, p1, kfb, k1 tog with wrap, w&t. 2 sts inc'd on right sleeve and 1 st inc'd on right front.

Short row 4 (WS): Purl to 1 st before m, k1, sl m, purl across right sleeve, sl m, k1, pfb, work Row 3 of chart over 44 (46, 48) sts, pfb, k1, sl m, p2, m1P, purl across left sleeve to 2 sts before m, m1P, p2, sl m, k1, pfb, p1 tog with wrap, w&t. 2 sts inc'd on back, 2 sts inc'd on left sleeve, and 1 st inc'd on left front.

Short row 5 (RS): Knit to 1 st before m, p1, sl m, knit across left sleeve, sl m, p1, work Row 4 of chart over 46 (48, 50) sts, p1, sl m, k2, m1L, knit across right sleeve to 2 sts before m, m1R, sl m, p1, kfb, knit to previously wrapped st, k st tog with wrap, w&t. 2 sts inc'd on right sleeve and 1 st inc'd on right front.

Short row 6 (WS): Purl to 1 st before m, k1, sl m, purl across right sleeve, sl m, k1, pfb, work Row 5 of chart over 46 (48, 50) sts, pfb, k1, sl m, p2, m1P, purl across left sleeve to 2 sts before m, m1P, p2, sl m, k1, pfb, purl to previously wrapped st, p st tog with wrap, w&t. 2 sts inc'd on back, 2 sts inc'd on left sleeve, and 1 st inc'd on left front.

Short row 7 (RS): Knit to 1 st before m, p1, sl m, knit across left sleeve, sl m, p1, work Row 6 of chart over 48 (50, 52) sts, p1, sl m, k2, m1L, knit across right sleeve to 2 sts before m, m1R, k2, sl m, p1, kfb, knit to previously wrapped st, k st tog with wrap, w&t. 2 sts inc'd on right sleeve and 1 st inc'd on right front.

Short row 8 (WS): Purl to 1 st before m, k1, sl m, purl across right sleeve, sl m, k1, pfb, work Row 7 of chart over 48 (50, 52) sts, pfb, k1, sl m, p2, m1P, purl across left sleeve to 2 sts before m, m1P, p2, sl m, k1, pfb, purl to previously wrapped st, p st tog with wrap, w&t. 2 sts inc'd on back, 2 sts inc'd on left sleeve, and 1 st inc'd on left front.

Short row 9 (RS): Knit to 1 st before m, p1, sl m, knit across left sleeve, sl m, p1, work Row 8 of chart over 50 (52, 54) sts, p1. 156 (164, 168) sts: 26 (28, 28) each sleeve, 52 (54, 56) each back and front.

Shape shoulders and begin cables on front and back: From this point to sleeve separation, poncho is worked in the round. Switch to longer circular needle when necessary. Cable Set-Up B chart will be worked on both back and front.

Rnd 1: Working rem wrapped sts tog with their wraps as you come to them, [k2, m1L, knit across sleeve to 2 sts before m, m1R, k2, sl m, p1, m1P, work Rnd 1 of Cable Set-Up B chart as indicated for your size over 50 (52, 54) sts, m1P, p1, sl m] 2 times. 164 (172, 176) sts: 28 (30, 30) each sleeve, 54 (56, 58) each back and front.

Rnd 2: [Knit across sleeve to m, sl m, p1, work Rnd 2 of chart over 52 (54, 56) sts, p1, sl m] 2 times.

Rnd 3: [Knit across sleeve to m, sl m, p1, m1P, work Rnd 3 of chart over 52 (54, 56) sts, m1P, p1, sl m] 2 times. 168 (176, 180) sts: 28 (30, 30) each sleeve, 56 (58, 60) each back and front.

Rnd 4: [Knit across sleeve to m, sl m, p1 (1, 2), work Rnd 4 of chart over 54 (56, 56) sts, p1 (1, 2), sl m] 2 times.

Rnd 5: [K2, m1L, knit across sleeve to 2 sts before m, m1R, k2, sl m, p1, m1P, p0 (0, 1), work Rnd 5 of chart over 54 (56, 56) sts, p0 (0, 1), m1P, p1, sl m] 2 times. 176 (184, 188) sts: 30 (32, 32) each sleeve, 58 (60, 62) each back and front.

Rnd 6: [Knit across sleeve to m, sl m, p1 (2, 3), pm for cable panel, work Rnd 6 of chart over 56 sts, pm for cable panel, p1 (2, 3), sl m] 2 times.

Rnd 7: [Knit across sleeve to m, sl m, p1, m1P, purl to cable panel m, sl m, work Rnd 7 of chart, sl m, purl to 1 st before m, m1P, p1, sl m] 2 times. 180 (188, 192) sts: 30 (32, 32) each sleeve, 60 (62, 64) each back and front.

Rnd 8: [Knit across sleeve to m, sl m, purl to cable panel m, sl m, work Rnd 8 of chart, sl m, purl to m, sl m] 2 times.

Shape body:
Rnd 1 (inc on back and front only): [Knit across sleeve to m, sl m, p1, m1P, purl to cable panel m, sl m, work Rnd 1 of Herringbone Cable Right over 12 sts, work Rnd 1 of Main Cable over 32 sts, work Rnd 1 of Herringbone Cable Left over 12 sts, sl m, purl to 1 st before m, m1P, p1, sl m] 2 times. 184 (192, 196) sts: 30 (32, 32) each sleeve, 62 (64, 66) each back and front.

Rnd 2: [Knit sleeve sts, sl m, purl to cable panel m, sl m, work next rnd of cables, sl m, purl to m, sl m] 2 times.

Rnd 3 (inc on back and front only): [Knit across sleeve to m, sl m, p1, m1P, purl to cable panel m, sl m, work next rnd of cables, sl m, purl to 1 st before m, m1P, p1, sl m] 2 times. 2 sts inc'd each back and front. 188 (196, 200) sts: 30 (32, 32) each sleeve, 64 (66, 68) each back and front.

Rnd 4: Rep Rnd 2.

Rnd 5 (inc on back/front and sleeves): [K2, m1L, knit across sleeve to 2 sts before m, m1R, k2, sl m, p1, m1P, purl to cable panel m, sl m, work next rnd of cables, sl m, purl to 1 st before m, m1P, p1, sl m] 2 times. 2 st inc'd each sleeve and 2 sts inc'd each back and front. 196 (204, 208) sts: 32 (34, 34) each sleeve, 66 (68, 70) each back and front.

Working in established patterns, continue to inc 2 sts on back and front on every 2nd rnd 0 (3, 17) more times, then on every 3rd rnd 25 (27, 20) times, and AT THE SAME TIME continue to inc 2 sts on each sleeve on every 6th rnd 7 (1, 2) more time(s), then on every – (7, 8)th rnd

0 (6, 5) times. When all incs are complete, there are 324 (352, 384) sts: 46 (48, 48) each sleeve and 116 (128, 144) each back and front.

Work even, if necessary, until poncho measures 15 (17, 18)" at center front from base of collar, or desired length; when tried on, bottom edge should fall just below waist and elbows.

Now each section will be finished separately, beginning with the right sleeve. Sleeve finishing adds 8" length to sleeve. Front and body finishing add 9.5 (10.5, 12)" of length at the longest point (center front/back) and 3.25" at sides. The St st part of the sleeve will be seamed to the side edges of the body at the end, so both pieces must be the same length. Accordingly, to lengthen sleeve, work extra rows in the ribbed cuff only, and to lengthen body add more short rows.

LOWER RIGHT SLEEVE

Row 1 (RS): CO 1 st on left needle, knit this st, then k46 (48, 48) sts to end of left sleeve section, remove m. Place front, left sleeve, and back sts on separate holders.

Row 2 (WS): CO 1 st on left needle, purl to end. 48 (50, 50) sts.

Row 3: Knit.

Row 4: K1, purl to last st, k1.

Dec row (RS): K2, ssk, knit to last 4 sts, k2tog, k2. 2 sts dec'd.

Continuing in St st with 1 garter st each end for selvedges, rep dec row on every 6th row 2 more times, then work 3 rows even. 42 (44, 44) sts rem.

Cuff:

Rib row: *K1, p1; rep from * to end. Rep this row until cuff measures 4.75". BO in rib.

LOWER FRONT

Note: The wrap and turn short rows here are not invisible, as they are worked close together and in reverse St st, but they are neat and tidy. Substitute your preferred short row method if desired.

Replace 116 (128, 144) held front sts on needle and join yarn with RS facing.

Row 1 (RS): CO 1 st on left needle, work in patt to end.

Row 2 (WS): CO 1 st on left needle, work in patt to end. 118 (130, 146) sts.

Short row shaping:

Short row 1 (RS): Work in patt to last 3 sts, w&t.

Short row 2 (WS): Work in patt to last 3 sts, w&t.

Short row 3: Work in patt to 1 st before previously wrapped st, w&t.

Rep the last row seventeen (21, 25) more times.

Short row 4: Work in patt to 2 sts before previously wrapped st, w&t.

Rep the last row 9 (11, 15) more times.

Short row 5: Work in patt to 4 sts before previously wrapped st, w&t.

Rep the last row 3 more times.

Short row 6 (RS): Work in patt to last 7 sts of Herringbone Cable Left, w&t. (If there is a cable crossing in the way of this w&t, work to last 9 sts of Cable instead.)

Short row 7 (WS): Work in patt to last 7 or last 9 sts (to correspond to previous row) of Herringbone Cable Right, w&t.

Short row 8: Work in patt to last st of Main Cable, w&t.

Rep the last row 1 more time.

Next row (RS): Work in patt to end, working wraps tog with wrapped sts.

Next row (WS): K1, m1P, work in patt to last st (working rem wraps tog with wrapped sts), m1P, k1.

Ribbed edge:

Rib row 1 (RS): K3, *p2, k2; rep from * to last st, k1.

Rib row 2: P3, *k2, p2; rep from * to last st, p1.

Rep these 2 rows until you have a total of 17 rows of ribbing.

BO all sts as follows: K1, *transfer 1 st from right needle to left, k2tog tbl; rep from * to end.

LOWER LEFT SLEEVE

Transfer held sts to needle, join yarn with RS facing and complete as for right sleeve.

LOWER BACK

Transfer held sts to needle, join yarn with RS facing and complete as for front.

FINISHING

Sew the 20 rows of each sleeve above the cuff to the free side edges of back and front. BO edge of back/front should align with top of cuff. Seam cuffs closed. Weave in ends and block. A good blocking will make the short rows much less noticeable and help the curved body ribbing to lie flat.

When you put poncho on, adjust sleeves so arms are not twisted, and give both front and back a tug down.

Cable Set-Up A

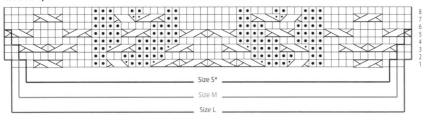

Herringbone Cable Right

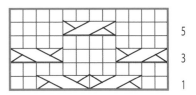

Cable Set-Up B

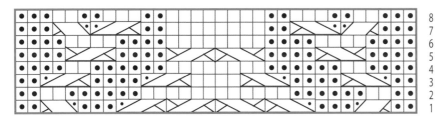

Herringbone Cable Left

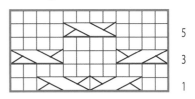

*On Rnd 5 where there are not enough sts to work the first and last cable crossings, knit these sts rather than work a partial cable.

Main Cable

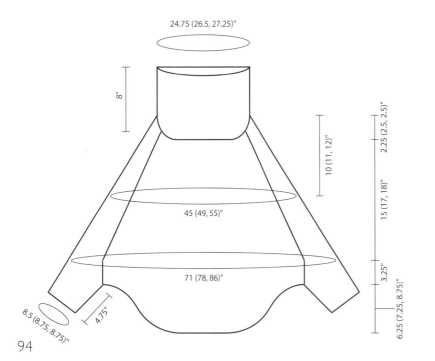

Key

- ☐ knit on RS, purl on WS
- • purl on RS, knit on WS
- ☐ pattern repeat
- sl 1 to cn and hold to back, k2, p1 from cn
- sl 2 to cn and hold to front, p1, k2 from cn
- RS: sl 2 to cn and hold to back, k2, k2 from cn
  WS: sl 2 to cn and hold to back, p2, p2 from cn
- RS: sl 2 to cn and hold to front, k2, k2 from cn
  WS: sl 2 to cn and hold to front, p2, p2 from cn
- sl 2 to cn and hold to back, k2, p2 from cn
- sl 2 to cn and hold to front, p2, k2 from cn

ABBREVIATIONS

BO   bind off, bound-off

Cn   cable needle

CO   cast on, cast-on

Dec('d) decrease(d)

Inc('d)   increase(d)

K   knit

Kfb   knit into front, then back of same st

K2tog   knit 2 sts together

M   marker

m1L   make 1 left: with right needle, pick up running thread between needles from back to front and place it on left needle, then knit it through the back loop

m1P   make 1 purl: with right needle, pick up running thread between needles from front to back, place on left needle, purl it through the front loop.

m1R   make 1 right: with right needle, pick up running thread between needles from front to back, place on left needle, knit it through the front loop

P   purl

Pfb   purl into front, then back of same st

Pm   place marker

Rem   remain

Rep   repeat

Rnd(s) round(s)

RS   right side

Sl   slip

Ssk   [sl 1 as if to knit] 2 times, insert left needle into these 2 sts and knit them together

St(s)   stitch(es)

St st   stockinette stitch

Tbl   through the back loop

Tog   together

W&t   wrap and turn (see Techniques)

WS   wrong side

TECHNIQUES

Wrap and Turn for Short Rows (w&t)

On a RS row: Slip the next st pwise wyib, bring yarn to front between needles, return slipped st to left needle, turn work.

On a WS row: Slip the next st pwise wyif, bring yarn to back between needles, return slipped st to left needle, turn work.

In the Kitchen: Owl Cookies

Since I was a little girl, making owl cookies always heralded the fall season in our household. The evenings would get cool and crisp, the leaves would start to turn, we would dig out the Halloween decorations . . . and then someone would say, "let's pick up cashews the next time we're at the grocery store" (cashews were not a regular menu item around our house at any other time of year).

I've continued the tradition with my three daughters, and they have enjoyed baking these cookies every fall to take to their friends and classmates. Their favorite part has always been putting on the eyes and noses – as a result, we always end up with at least a few owls that have gone cross-eyed or wall-eyed!

Ingredients:

1 cup butter	1 tsp baking powder
1 ½ cups sugar	1 tsp salt
4 tsp vanilla	2 one-ounce squares unsweetened chocolate (melted)
2 eggs	chocolate chips
3 ½ cups flour	cashews

Cream together butter, sugar and vanilla; beat in eggs. Add dry ingredients. Divide dough in half. Add melted chocolate to one half. Place balls of dough into two separate pieces of wax paper and refrigerate until stiff and easy to handle without sticking.

On waxed paper, roll out vanilla half of dough into a rectangle approx. 6" wide. Roll chocolate half into a long snake, 1-2" thick and the same length as the vanilla rectangle. Place chocolate snake on top of vanilla rectangle (rectangle still on wax paper) and starting along one of the long ends, begin rolling, pressing vanilla to chocolate to eliminate any air gaps. Refrigerate first if too sticky. When done, you will have a long tube of chocolate inside vanilla. Wrap the sides of the wax paper around the tube and chill until stiff and not too sticky to handle.

Slice the roll in ½-inch pieces. Place on silicone cookie sheet in pairs, with centers pressed together. Pinch tops for ears. Place chocolate chips for eyes and cashews for noses. Bake at 375 degrees for 8-10 minutes. ⌘

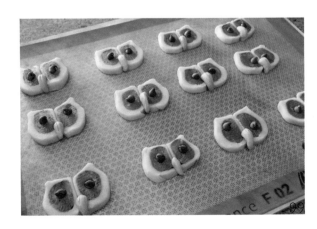

Wildlife can be found everywhere on the islands in Puget Sound, including this bald eagle (left), sighted on Bainbridge Island fishing for an evening supper, or this quail (below left), keeping a wary eye out for danger on Whidbey Island. Wild rabbits are everywhere in the town of Langley on Whidbey Island. We stopped counting at 100!

Personal Patchwork: Wise Craft Handmade

Blair Stocker's professional career had always revolved around fabric—her college degree and post-college employment focused on apparel and fabric design—but she'd never tried quilting until she had children. "I was always super creative in my job, but I left it all at work. I didn't have the time or the energy to be creative outside of work. Then, when I started staying home once my kids were born, the void of not having the creative outlet at work pushed me to find something that I really enjoyed doing at home." Blair decided to make a quilt out of her daughter's baby clothes. "Nobody in my family quilted. I didn't know anything about quilting. All I knew was that you sew little pieces of fabric together."

From the very beginning, Blair's quilts focused on reusing fabrics that were already imbued with meaning. "The idea of buying new fabric to cut it up and put it into a quilt didn't make sense to me." So she used pieces of her daughter's baby clothes and pieced them together for the quilt front, and used a crib sheet for the backing. "I didn't even care if I did it right, I just wanted to create this memory for her."

Around the same time, Blair began blogging, which "developed this really rich community with other creative people doing what I was doing—staying at home in the intense days of raising children, but finding time to be creative and having a place to record it and talk about it." She began to put more of her time and effort into learning about quilting. "I was fascinated by the idea that quilts can be composed. It's not just that you're cutting up fabrics and piecing them in a patchwork, you can actually compose a larger, comprehensive design."

Many of the quilts in Blair's studio workroom have been assembled from unexpected materials. One is made from blocks of thrifted felted sweaters. Another is made from pieces of ski parkas, and yet another is constructed from different denim fabrics. One of my favorites is created from pieces of men's dress shirts; one of the blocks has even left the pocket on, convenient for tucking in a favorite stuffed animal or treasure.

"The reason I find it so interesting to use thrifted materials is that so many new fabrics come in collections that are already chosen for you. Upcycling or using vintage materials means that the maker is really doing the curating. You're putting thought into what is included – or not." Her recently published book, *Wise Craft Quilts*, walks readers through using special collections of fabric that have meaning or memories for the maker. "Or, if you have memories that aren't linked to particular fabric, you can create memories on fabric." Blair showed me an example of this type of quilt: her family embroidered funny sayings or inside jokes on each block (see above right).

Blair's love of working with "memories fabric" has inspired the publication of several books. The first, titled *Wise Craft: Turning Thrift Store Finds, Fabric Scraps, and Natural Objects into Stuff You Love*, is described on the Wise Craft website as a primer for "turning forgotten cast-offs, outgrown clothing, and other things into special new objects that enhance your living space and tell your story." Just this year, Blair published *Wise Craft Quilts: A Guide to Turning Beloved Fabrics into Meaningful Patchwork*. These quilts are described as those "that celebrate our family, memories, and special moments in our lives . . . the memories they evoke, and the stories they tell, become

quilts that have souls. These quilts are meant to be out in our homes and used every day. To make us smile and keep us warm, literally and metaphorically."

In addition to two published books and several self-published patterns, Blair teaches classes in the Seattle area at Drygoods Design and at quilting guilds. "The only downside to teaching in person is that I do not get to see the finished quilts." To create this sense of completion from start to finish of a quilting project, Blair's next endeavor is to create an online community through a six-week virtual class. "It's called *Dream, Learn, Quilt*: two weeks of dreaming up your project, two weeks of learning the steps, and two weeks of doing the actual quilting. In between, I'm going to give them everything they need to know to take the project to completion." Blair's goal is to "be very present" with her students through Facebook Live and Q&A videos. "I think there's always been a community around quilting, and a desire for community – that's what led to the formation of guilds. In preparing for this class, I wanted it to feel like a quilting bee, where we are all there to support each other and bounce ideas off each other." ⌘

Wise Craft Handmade

Quilter: Blaire Stocker

Website: wisecrafthandmade.com

Instagram: blairs

Books: "Wise Craft" and "Wise Craft Quilts"

Products: Quilt patterns, custom-made quilts, online and in-person classes

By Hand Author and Photographer

Andrea Hungerford is an obsessive knitter who lives with her husband, three daughters and three cats, a Great Pyrenees farm dog, and a variety of chickens and rabbits on acreage outside of Portland, Oregon. Andrea's "mini-farm" affords her the opportunity to grow vegetables, berries, fruit trees, and cutting flowers. After working for more than twenty years as an attorney, Andrea finds peace and joy in working with her hands. She has never met a hand craft that doesn't intrigue her, and her current repertoire of making includes sewing, quilting, embroidery, mosaics, hand thrown pottery, canning, candlemaking, photography, and anything involving fiber and fabric. Her heart, however, belongs to knitting, and she can often be found during the summer in a corner of her garden, or in the winter in front of the fireplace in her parlor, with her latest knitting project flying off her needles.

Karen DeWitz lives in the woods just outside of Oregon City with her husband, teenage son (whose older brother is away at college), and a rambunctious fluffy dog. Karen was a teacher for ten years and then edited math textbooks for many more before turning full-time to her two great passions: photography and great books. (She kept her amateur status in her other favorite pastimes: hiking and drinking coffee.) She loves to photograph common things in new or evocative ways and is always looking for interesting angles, contrasts of light, or unusual patterns in everyday moments. She spends way more time than she should admit photographing birds and raindrops in her yard. When she's not taking pictures or chasing after her escape-artist dog, Karen also edits YA and middle grade novels.

Upcoming Issues

Upcoming issues of **By Hand** will feature different makers' communities around the country, such as:

- Lake Michigan
- North Carolina
- British Columbia
- Rocky Mountains
- Hudson Valley
- Northern California

If you have suggestions for an artist or maker, a knitting store or small business, or anything unique in these locations, we'd love to hear from you! Do you know of a makers' community that you think we should profile? If so, let us know! Email us at: info@byhandserial.com.

You can also find us on:
Ravelry at www.ravelry.com/groups/by-hand-serial
Facebook at www.facebook.com/byhandserial
Instagram at www.instagram.com/byhandserial